New Directions for
Community Colleges

Arthur M. Cohen
EDITOR-IN-CHIEF

Caroline Q. Durdella
Nathan R. Durdella
ASSOCIATE EDITORS

Amy Fara Edwards
MANAGING EDITOR

Bringing College Education Into Prisons

Robert Scott
EDITOR

D1523522

Number 170 • Summer 2015
Jossey-Bass
San Francisco

BRINGING COLLEGE EDUCATION INTO PRISONS
Robert Scott (ed.)
New Directions for Community Colleges, no. 170

Arthur M. Cohen, Editor-in-Chief
Caroline Q. Durdella, Nathan R. Durdella, Associate Editors
Amy Fara Edwards, Managing Editor

NEW DIRECTIONS FOR COMMUNITY COLLEGES (ISSN 0194-3081, electronic ISSN 1536-0733) is part of The Jossey-Bass Higher and Adult Education Series and is published quarterly by Wiley Subscription Services, Inc., A Wiley Company, at Jossey-Bass, One Montgomery St., Ste. 1200, San Francisco, CA 94104. POSTMASTER: Send address changes to New Directions for Community Colleges, Jossey-Bass, One Montgomery St., Ste. 1200, San Francisco, CA 94104.

SUBSCRIPTIONS cost $89 for individuals in the U.S., Canada, and Mexico, and $113 in the rest of the world for print only; $89 in all regions for electronic only; $98 in the U.S., Canada, and Mexico for combined print and electronic; $122 for combined print and electronic in the rest of the world. Institutional print only subscriptions are $335 in the U.S., $375 in Canada and Mexico, and $409 in the rest of the world; electronic only subscriptions are $335 in all regions; combined print and electronic subscriptions are $402 in the U.S., $442 in Canada and Mexico, and $476 in the rest of the world.

Cover design: Wiley
Cover Images: © Lava 4 images | Shutterstock

EDITORIAL CORRESPONDENCE should be sent to the Editor-in-Chief, Arthur M. Cohen, at 1749 Mandeville Lane, Los Angeles, CA 90049. All manuscripts receive anonymous reviews by external referees.

New Directions for Community Colleges is indexed in CIJE: Current Index to Journals in Education (ERIC), Contents Pages in Education (T&F), Current Abstracts (EBSCO), Ed/Net (Simpson Communications), Education Index/Abstracts (H. W. Wilson), Educational Research Abstracts Online (T&F), ERIC Database (Education Resources Information Center), and Resources in Education (ERIC).

Microfilm copies of issues and articles are available in 16mm and 35mm, as well as microfiche in 105mm, through University Microfilms Inc., 300 North Zeeb Road, Ann Arbor, MI 48106-1346.

CONTENTS

EDITOR'S NOTES

On June 11, 2014, 60 incarcerated men took an entrance exam for placement into an associate's degree program in a prison in New York. They were asked to list any past college experience on their cover sheet; one man wrote, "Corning Community College at Elmira, 1995." In the wider world, one might ask what had prevented this individual from completing his associate's degree 20 years earlier—but in the prison context, the reference to 1995 is revealing.

Elmira refers to Elmira Correctional Facility (a prison in New York), and 1995 was the year its community college program was closed. In 1994, the Federal Crime Bill restricted the provision of Pell grants to incarcerated people, which was the sole source of funding for community colleges in prison. By the end of 1995, which happened to be this man's second year in prison, the majority of the college programs in prison were gone—not just in New York, but across the country. Thus, like so many men in New York prisons, the man encountered in 2014 had not completed his associate's degree, nor had he transferred to a four-year institution. Instead, he was still seeking an opportunity to complete his first semester of college. His academic transcripts now document a 20-year gap in college access that resulted from the 1994 law. Once he passed the entrance exam in 2014, he was allowed to continue where he left off, adding to the nine credits he received two decades earlier, now in the final months of his sentence before he is eligible for parole. Only this time, the state was not supporting his college expenses—post-1995 programs have created new means to bring college education into prison rather than wait for the return of state funding.

This volume of *New Directions for Community Colleges* engages the experiences of community college instructors working in America's prisons today, 20 years after the denial of Pell support to incarcerated students. There are fewer programs today than there were in 1994 (see Table 1, and Figures 1 and 2). The programs of 2014 have each had to discover new means to fund themselves, although many would suggest that the economic impact of such programs is offset by the reduced costs of reincarceration through successful reentry. Almost everyone in prison returns to the community they came from, and a community college education can make the difference between gainful employment and unemployment, a path to productive citizenship among various opportunities to return to a life of crime. The role of community college in providing ladders of opportunity goes back to the origins of the junior college; today's college-in-prison

NEW DIRECTIONS FOR COMMUNITY COLLEGES, no. 170, Summer 2015 © 2015 Wiley Periodicals, Inc.
Published online in Wiley Online Library (wileyonlinelibrary.com) • DOI: 10.1002/cc.20138

Table 1.   Community Colleges in New York State Prisons When
Incarcerated Students Could Receive Pell Grants (up to 1994) and
20 Years After Pell Grants Were Taken Away

1994: 13 Community Colleges in 31 New York State Prisons
Bronx Community College (Sing Sing)
Cayuga Community College (Auburn, Cayuga)
Clinton Community College (Altona, Lyon Mountain)
Columbia-Greene Community College (Hudson)
Corning Community College (Elmira)
Dutchess Community College (Beacon, Fishkill, Green Haven)
Genesee Community College (Albion, Attica, Groveland, Orleans)
Jefferson Community College (Gouverneur, Watertown)
Mohawk Valley Community College (Marcy, Mohawk, Mid-State, Oneida)
North Country Community College (Adirondack, Bare Hill, Franklin)
Sage Junior College of Albany (Coxsackie, Green, Mt. McGregor)
Sullivan County Community College (Sullivan, Woodbourne)
Ulster County Community College (Eastern, Shawangunk, Wallkill)

2014: 5 Community Colleges in 5 New York State Prisons
Cayuga Community College (Auburn)*
Genesee Community College (Attica)
Mohawk Valley Community College (Mohawk)*
Jefferson Community College (Cape Vincent)
Sullivan County Community College (Sullivan)*

*Of the five community colleges involved today, three are partnering with four-year colleges.

educators are particularly motivated by the dramatic growth of the prison system and the disproportionate incarceration of African-Americans and Latinos some 50 years after the Civil Rights Act.

The United States has the largest prison population, both proportionately and in absolute terms, of any society in the history of the world (Carson, 2014). We live in what has been referred to as "the era of mass incarceration." The 2.3 million people incarcerated in the United States do not draw equally from all sectors of society: African-Americans and Latino/as are more likely than Whites to be sent to prison, even when found guilty of committing the same crimes. The policing of people of color, specifically Black men, has recently gained public attention via sensational media stories, and the preponderance of African-American men in U.S. prisons is a prominent theme in the chapters that follow. This is intuitive, for the sheer scale of mass incarceration has converted prison into a latent mechanism by which non-White people are denied access to higher education. For example, in one year there were 992 African-American men who received bachelor's degrees from Illinois state universities, while roughly 7,000 African-American men were released from Illinois state prisons just for drug offenses alone (Alexander, 2010, p. 185).

I was motivated to organize this volume of *New Directions for Community Colleges* by a desire to share the experiences of community college

Figure 1. Map of Prison Higher Education in New York State, Spring 1994

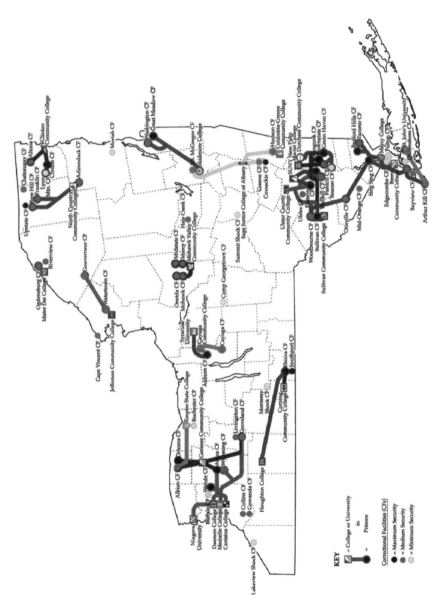

KEY

◻ = College or University
in
◼ = Prisons

Correctional Facilities (CFs)

● = Maximum Security
● = Medium Security
● = Minimum Security

Figure 2.   Map of Prison Higher Education in New York State, Spring 2014

educators in establishing and maintaining college programs in prison during this historical moment. The contributing authors write of the inspiring resilience of their incarcerated students, the programmatic innovations that made it possible to bring college education into prison, and most importantly what educators around the country can do right now to reconnect community colleges with nearby citizens behind bars. Many of these authors touch upon the constraints of working inside prisons—for instance, the real or perceived hostility of prison employees to those who enter prisons temporarily with a mission of education and social uplift. Others highlight how the social structure within prison, which is enacted by the incarcerated population, impacts the classroom. A few authors also describe the specific steps by which their community college developed a program in recent years, given the scarcity of financial resources.

Partnerships between community colleges and four-year colleges and universities have fueled the recent growth of college-in-prison programs, and much of this volume of *New Directions* focuses on the collaboration and learning between partnering institutions working inside prison walls. At the time that I proposed the idea for this sourcebook, I was working for both a state university and a community college that offered courses in a prison in Illinois. The community college provided an associate's degree program, and the university enrolled graduates of the program in upper-division (third and fourth year) courses with the hope of offering a bachelor's degree—I say hope because, like many of the programs around the country, this initiative was fairly new, and there were considerable challenges encountered in launching a degree program without state support. This is all to say that bringing college education into prison is a work in progress, and this sourcebook contains a collection of insights and experiences from educators who are bringing these programs back into existence.

Our volume begins with an essay that both articulates the need for prison education and describes a mechanism to fund new community college programs inside prison walls. Doran Larson draws thoughtful comparisons between the U.S. prison system and its counterparts in Northern Europe, then goes on to explain a low-cost mechanism to fund community college programs today by mimicking the dual credit arrangements that are set up for high school students. The second chapter is a case study of the creation of a community college program inside of a correctional facility, written by Betsy Simpkins. Her chapter answers many basic questions facing a community college operating a program inside a prison: What is the rationale? How does a community college program in prison work? How are students recruited and selected? How does one communicate with the Department of Corrections? The remainder of the volume provides many variations on these introductory themes.

The following three chapters engage student voices from inside prison walls. In Chapter 3, Jenifer D. Drew, José Duval, and James R. Cyr describe a successful four-semester Spanish curriculum that was made possible against the odds due to enlisting tutors from within the incarcerated population at a prison in Massachusetts. In Chapter 4, Lee Ragsdale describes a similar program from a community college in Illinois, and coauthor Erick Nava Palomino reflects on the empowerment of the experience from his new home in Mexico, where he now works as a language instructor. Chapter 5 switches gears as Daniel E. Graves warns us from within prison walls of the threat of corruption that community colleges face when hosting courses on the inside. He tells us that institutional pressure to graduate as many people as possible can combine with a culture of nondisclosure of misconduct to create the conditions for low-quality education to go undetected, due to the walled-off nature of prison life.

The next three chapters dive into questions of pedagogy with respect to the specific populations found in prison settings. In Chapter 6, Nathaniel B. D. Moore describes his experience teaching African history in the heavily racialized and segregated space of a California state prison. The themes of his chapter are echoed by Tony Gaskew in Chapter 7, as both authors call for curricular content that reflects the specific racial and ethnic interests of the prison population. Gaskew develops an entire pedagogical model he terms the "Humiliation to Humility Perspective," which employs an Afrocentric education to directly confront the reality of challenges that lay before African-American men, who are disproportionately incarcerated in the era of mass incarceration. In Chapter 8, Jane Maher introduces us to the particularities of teaching writing in a women's prison; she reflects on the various assignment and readings she has selected over the years, and how they worked in the all-female context.

The final two chapters address broader questions of how to understand and use community college to address the issue of prison in the era of mass incarceration. In Chapter 9, Larry Brewster describes the vivid space of transformation that opens up when education in the fine arts are engaged in prison. Art is crucial to prison education; creative expression is not only potentially therapeutic but at the same time it holds the potential to enable radical critique and commentary on the system, engaging multiple intelligences and conserving creativity in a prison context that otherwise tends to diminish the variety of human potential. Finally, in Chapter 10, Mary Rachel Gould, Gillian Harkins, and Kyes Stevens discuss the civic engagement implicit in prison teaching, and ask us to think of prison education in a participatory framework rather than the more common service-oriented model. Rather than end on a note of resolution, their essay reminds us that the work proposed in this sourcebook is problematic, and that the answer to mass incarceration is not only more education but decarceration.

Robert Scott
Editor

NEW DIRECTIONS FOR COMMUNITY COLLEGES • DOI: 10.1002/cc

References

Alexander, M. (2010). *The new Jim Crow: Mass incarceration in the age of colorblindness.* New York, NY: The New Press.
Carson, E. A. (2014, September). Prisoners in 2013. *Bulletin of the Bureau of Justice Statistics.* Washington, DC: United States Department of Justice.

ROBERT SCOTT *is the executive director of the Cornell Prison Education Program at Cornell University.*

1

This chapter describes methods for funding community programs in prison in the context of national and international political economy of mass incarceration.

Localizing Prison Higher Education

Doran Larson

Every dollar invested in the education and training of incarcerated people returns five dollars in savings to state coffers (Davis, Bozick, Steele, Saunders, & Miles, 2013). The benefits of such investment are also naturally expansive. Returning more job-ready men and women to our most troubled communities helps brake the ghetto-to-prison revolving door that has helped to build the largest prison complex on earth (Page, 2004; Wacquant, 2000). Among the 720,000 men and women who leave prisons and jails each year in the United States, more than two thirds are reincarcerated within three years after release, and over three quarters after five years from release (Cooper, Durose, & Snyder, 2014). Every person who leaves prison with an associate's degree is approximately 75% more likely to avoid reincarceration, less likely to victimize others, and more likely to be able to support families inside the legitimate economy and thus to break the generational cycle of incarceration that plagues up to 70% of the children of imprisoned people (Christian, 2009; Parke & Clarke-Stewart, 2002; Patillo, Weiman, & Western, 2004; Schirmer, Ashley, & Marc, 2009). If we bracket the charged (and, for the past 40 years, politically exploited) question of who "deserves" rehabilitative services and take a purely utilitarian view of the prison-education policies that best secure public safety, reduce tax rolls, and help poor communities regain their human capital, there is no viable argument *against* higher education for incarcerated people.

But we cannot afford to be unrealistic about such questions. When, in a primary debate, Governor Rick Perry drew cheers for his authorization of 234 executions in Texas, he tapped into the vein of penal populism that since 1973 has effectively turned much of U.S. criminal justice policy and practice away from offering detached, research-based arbitration of the greatest good for the greatest number in dealing with lawbreakers and into a state-sponsored apparatus of public vengeance. The opposition evoked by Governor Andrew Cuomo's 2014 proposal that New York

NEW DIRECTIONS FOR COMMUNITY COLLEGES, no. 170, Summer 2015 © 2015 Wiley Periodicals, Inc.
Published online in Wiley Online Library (wileyonlinelibrary.com) • DOI: 10.1002/cc.20139

State help fund college-in-prison programs (Bakeman, 2014) demonstrates that antiprisoner sentiment confronts even modest moves toward making prisons into truly correctional institutions. Politicians opposed to such funding called the proposal "incredible," "shocking," and "insulting" to law-abiding students, and "simply beyond belief" ("Republicans," 2014). Yet such programs—funded by the states and the federal government—had operated nationwide just two decades earlier. Until 1994, when Bill Clinton signed legislation making prisoners ineligible, one tenth of one percent (0.1%) of all Pell grants funded more than 350 college-in-prison programs across the country. Yet the opposition that Cuomo's modest proposal evoked suggested that such funding had never been imagined by anyone, anywhere, at any time. As welcome as state and federal funding would be, it will continue to come and go with the political winds. (Penal populism and mass incarceration have enjoyed thoroughly bipartisan support.) The issue, however, is not whether the public wants to see a reduction in prison populations that cost taxpayers $75 billion a year (Schmitt, Warner, & Gupta, 2010). The touchy issue is what we do with prisoners *while* they are incarcerated. Even conservatives recognize that we are paying too much for incarceration numbers, far beyond what is required by public safety (Reddy & Levin, 2013). Over half the states and the justice department are revising mandatory sentencing; many are developing drug and mental health courts that sentence offenders to treatment rather than prison time. Others, aided by the 2008 Bush administration Second Chance Act, focus on reentry: putting in place the supports that ex-offenders need in order to stay out of prison. The political third rail in this case is what happens to incarcerated people while in prison—during years when a vocal part of the public believes, and prison-invested politicians have claimed, that prisoners have one proper occupation: to suffer state-sponsored punishment.

Based upon the evidence of the value and savings to all citizens of prison higher education, yet realistic about both an economy that now depends upon the tax-funded make-work project of excess incarceration (the nation's third largest employer across all sectors and levels of criminal justice work; Wacquant, 2009) and current antiprisoner state and federal politics this chapter looks at one effort to create a new paradigm for *who is responsible for* incarcerated Americans while serving prison time. This is a paradigm taken in part from European models but adapted to the American penal landscape. I'll begin with an outline, in very broad strokes, of penal practices in Northern Europe.

Adapting European to U.S. Penal Practice

Nordic prisons base policy and practice on *normalization*: If prison time is to prepare for reassimilation into life outside, this can best be achieved by making life inside as much like life outside as possible. Part of this normalization is achieved by connecting prisoners with the local community outside prison walls: public-school education is provided not by prison-service employees but by local educators who agree to work inside; medical personnel also come from the outside—with the qualifications and standards expected by the public—rather than, as we do in the United States, having the prison hire the least able of medical providers (Chang, 2012); the same is true for clergy, vocational trainers, and the like. Nordic prisoners establish and maintain contacts with people in the world outside, where they can continue supportive contact when they leave prison (Directorate of Norwegian Criminal Service, n.d.; Larson, 2013; Pratt, 2013). This is possible because Nordic incarceration rates are extremely low—about 10% of those in the United States—and prisons are small (Walmsley, 2011). Prisoners can be housed in or very near the communities they come from. The doctors, teachers, and clergy they meet inside are those they will meet as neighbors and mentors outside.

We know that continued contact with family and home communities is a primary factor in motivating ex-offenders to stay out of prison (Minnesota Department of Corrections, 2011). Yet the United States practices geographic exile as part of its punishment regime. Prisons have been offered as make-work gifts to rural, predominantly White communities, whose political representatives are the first to attack college programs that not only threaten prison longevity by reducing recidivism but also threaten to redraw districts determined by counting prisoners into local populations, even though U.S. prisoners cannot vote. It is as unrealistic to imagine prisons inviting in local service providers with whom ex-offenders might maintain constructive relationships outside as it is to expect incarcerated families—who are overwhelmingly poor and urban—to travel regularly to visit their loved ones upstate. European-style normalization is simply unrealistic given the geographic realities of U.S. incarceration. What we can adapt from European models is the localization of *responsibility* for prison service, reform, and higher education, and we can do this anywhere we find a viable geographic proximity between a prison, a community college, and other institutions of higher education.

The Idea in Practice

In 2009, with funding from a private philanthropic foundation, I began organizing a community college program, leading to an associate's degree granted by Genesee Community College (GCC), inside Attica Correctional Facility, in western New York. The Attica-Genesee Teaching Project (AGTP), with full tuition paid by the foundation to GCC since January 2011, has supported GCC faculty who offer four courses per semester enrolling 15 incarcerated students each. Though I teach today at a private, four-year institution, my first full-time appointment was at a two-year campus of the University of Wisconsin system. There I witnessed firsthand the organic relationship that community colleges bear to the communities where they stand, the commitment of community college administrators to local service, and the hard work contributed by community college faculty who provide the first step up for the majority of those first-generation students who seek to improve their condition. Though Attica has a well-earned reputation as a hard, punishing institution, the facility offered a willing superintendent, deputy superintendent for programs, and academic education supervisor, all working under a state commissioner who was a tireless advocate for higher education inside. Over half the Attica population of 2,200 men sent written notice of interest in the program (contrary to popular belief that incarcerated people who seek education inside are the exceptions), and 880 of these held a high school diploma or GED. The then-president of GCC wanted to renew the legacy of providing college courses inside Attica that he had initiated in 1972—after the bloody uprising of 1971—and had been forced to end in 1994 when Pell grant funding was withdrawn. He assigned the AGTP's day-to-day operations, curricular planning, and faculty recruitment to a dean so efficient in her work that the program expanded after its first two years—from offering three courses to twelve men each, each semester, to offering four, fifteen-student courses—without increasing its total annual budget. The bulk of this savings came from appealing to publishers for donations of the required texts.

What impressed me most powerfully over the course of two years of meetings, e-mails, and telephone calls involved in creating the AGTP was the depth of goodwill and breadth of vision among all of these people and offices. However myopic and mired in antiprisoner resentment and assumptions the conversation at the state and federal levels might be, at the local level, among prison and education administrators and academic staff, there was virtually no need to make the case for such a program. Goodwill and responsible, practical thinking existed in the key places where it was needed. Faculty who teach in the AGTP keep asking to teach at Attica again because the men there are so thoroughly engaged, prepared, and hardworking (both despite and due to having no access to the Internet, a library that hardly deserves the name, and no calculators). Yet none of the conversations leading to the now–three and a half years of successful curricular offerings would have taken place had I not brought the promise of full tuition funding. The question in my mind was whether it might be possible to recruit enough goodwill to obviate the need for so much funding support. Was it possible to create a program that pooled enough institutional volunteerism to reduce costs to a level that the *local community* might viably assume? Could local actors create a program independent from both the political winds that buffet state and federal funding (a theoretical independence, since no such funding is available), and from charitable foundations that not only deal with an excess of need and the instability of capital markets but whose very missions have become entwined with venture capitalist thinking and may be as volatile (Jacobson, 2013; "Venture Philanthropy," 2013)? A consortium model might not "normalize" prison experience for those inside, but it might normalize linkages between local public and private educational institutions and the prisons where local people earn their salaries and wages, and thus from which they support the local economies upon which institutions of higher education rely. The aim was to act toward prisons as a community responsibility, detached from shortsighted state and federal political debates that feed on the same ugly populism that fueled the creation of mass incarceration in the first place.

In January 2014, the Mohawk Consortium College-in-Prison Program (MCC) began delivering two 12-student sections of English 101 and one 13-student class in introductory biology at Mohawk Correctional Facility, a medium-security prison in central New York. The MCC will offer one summer course and three courses in the fall. The consortium institutions are Mohawk Valley Community College, Colgate University, and Hamilton College. The total first-year budget will be $30,000—half the cost of holding one person in prison in New York State for one year (Henrichson & Delaney, 2012). The savings to taxpayers, if numbers from past experience hold and the program reduces the recidivism rate for these 37 men by 75%, will be $1,887,000 for *each year* after their release. (This is savings in repeat incarceration costs alone. It does not include the tax contributions these men might make once employed, nor the savings realized by reducing the likelihood that their children will go to prison.) To break the fixed-sum, either/or thinking that pits the price tag to educate imprisoned people against the struggles of free-world students to meet rising tuition costs, this savings could potentially provide 157 free-world students free tuition to complete an associate's degree. Like the AGTP, the MCC exists because of the engaged professionalism, flexibility, and creativity of local actors: a community college president with a deep sense of community service; community college and private college staff, administrators, and faculty; and the correctional facility's very supportive superintendent, deputy superintendent for programs, and academic supervisor. The key to maintaining such low program costs and thus high potential social return is local, private college contributions of faculty under the community college's program of "dual credit."

The Administrative Key

Many community colleges offer dual credit to high school students. Qualified high school teachers (holding a master's degree or beyond) can offer courses in which students earn both credit toward their high school diplomas and credits toward an associate's degree or, eventually, a four-year degree. The student pays no added tuition, since high school faculty teach these classes. Mohawk Valley Community College (MVCC) is the administrative and curricular home of the MCC. MVCC administrators agreed to extend the dual credit model (though only one form of credit is offered) to incarcerated students. Community college tuition costs are zero for all correctional-facility students enrolled in courses delivered by faculty not normally employed by MVCC. Deans at Colgate and Hamilton have each agreed—as an act of good community will and public engagement—to offer one course release each year (on full salary) to a faculty member willing to teach in the MCC. The labor contract covering MVCC staff stipulates that MVCC faculty have first choice of any courses offered as part of the MVCC curriculum. When they do choose to teach in the MCC, full community-college tuition costs must be covered. The $30,000-a-year budget is, in effect, a contingency fund to cover those courses that MVCC faculty choose to offer, as well as books (though the textbooks for the first semester were donated after appeals to publishers, with the cost of one title covered by a single, private donation). Paper and other personal supplies are purchased by prisoners from the prison commissary—a policy that the prison administration imposes in order that imprisoned people invest in their own education. In theory, the MCC could operate with a much smaller budget than it does now. Costs will fluctuate from semester to semester as MVCC (on the cost side) and private college faculty (on the savings side) feel more enthused about and seek to get involved with prison teaching. (Oversight of the program, curricular planning, and arranging course logistics are handled in conversation between the head of academic education at the facility, the head of community education at MVCC, myself, and others as called for.) Yet the funding now provided to the MCC by a private foundation is so modest that, after a pilot grant period of four years, such funding might be assumed collectively by the participating institutions or by local granting agencies.

A Historic Moment

Prison higher education can change and literally save the lives of incarcerated people. Educators and administrators should also be mindful of the enormous service that local action yields to the nation at large. The prison and jail population outnumbers our fourth largest city, but it is spread across the same broad map that community colleges serve. When 60% of Black male high school dropouts will see the inside of a prison cell by age 35 (Western, 2006), and we know that higher education can help imprisoned people not return to prison, the service that community colleges provide as a matter of course is the service most desperately needed on what many today consider the most pressing civil rights front of our time. Faculty and administrators who go into prisons to help incarcerated people change the trajectories of their lives are among today's most vital, frontline civil rights workers.

This is a historic moment—one in which we are offered the chance to dismantle the state of de facto penal apartheid that sees whole cohorts of poor people of color swept up into prisons and jails, largely for nonviolent drug crimes perpetrated at higher rates among middle-class Whites (Alexander, 2010; Knafo, 2013). Equally important, the singular genius of community college expertise in quietly engaging and creating synergies between local resources and people of all races, classes, and political persuasions can remove the debate on prison higher education from the decidedly low level of politicized and highly emotional and misinformed demagoguery that rages whenever discussion of state or federal funding for prison higher education arises. Community colleges, which serve the same communities supported by a tax base fed by the salaries and wages paid to prison workers, and where formerly incarcerated people are most likely to seek their education—while sitting beside the children of prison workers— are the natural, honest brokers for new thinking about the relations between prisons, institutions of higher education, and the community at large.

Today, community colleges link education and the economic health of local communities at the same time that elite colleges and even four-year state universities are retreating from this role, since these institutions are chasing more out-of-state tuition dollars in order to make up for loss of state funding (Woodhouse, 2012). These increasingly noncommunity institutions draw students from and send them home to other regions, states, and nations. Community colleges are not only the natural but the *most experienced and able* institutions for transforming a state and national problem— mass incarceration—into a local conversation about who is responsible for the rehabilitation, education, and training of prisoners whose presence in the community, though behind prison walls, brings state and federal dollars to local communities. With their frontline experience in the work that distinguishes American higher education from higher education in other developed nations—making higher education accessible to all citizens, of any age or condition, at affordable costs—community colleges can also help elite, private institutions break through the walls and razor wire of high tuition and obsessive attention given exclusively to competitor institutions far from the local community. Elite institutions need community colleges today in order to see the way to true (that is, locally networked and sustained) public service. High-priced private colleges too often serve what is, in effect, an exclusionary purpose: seeing that the children of some rich people meet and bond with the children of other rich people and keep themselves at the front of the line for the most desirable jobs and careers (Espenshade, 2013). In its knowledge of and commitment to serving the local community—including the prison workers whose tax dollars support the same roads and schools and civil infrastructure that elite-institution faculty and administrators and students rely upon every day—the community college can show neighboring institutions the way to treating and remedying, locally, the same state and national prison crisis that many elite college and university faculty build careers by analyzing, theorizing, and critiquing. Community colleges are the natural venue and the wise counselors through which elite college faculty who write and theorize about inequalities driven by race and class can actually address inequality on its most pressing front (rather than simply pursuing diversity through rainbow representation of the children of the affluent among non-Whites).

The Mohawk Consortium makes clear that by working with the practical expertise, the administrative creativity, and the commitment of community colleges to local service, elite colleges can be engaged in paying back some of the debt they owe to the prisoners who are unlikely ever to appear on their campuses, but who also bring the infrastructure-supporting tax dollars that elite colleges need in order to serve their affluent clientele. The financial savings realized by states that host such collaborative efforts might then be committed to lowering the costs of public higher education. This would give the public reason to support and cheer on prisoners' academic success rather than reason to resent it. The result: Educated prisoners return to their communities as contributors to the health, safety, and economic stability of troubled neighborhoods; all aspiring students get a better shot at an affordable education; inequality on the ground is reduced.

Everything described here has been done and can be practiced more widely. The political will is all that's wanting—or the intelligence to do these things below the political radar, where sensible people, bound by the community college's mission of public service, can see the complementarity of their aspirations, their needs, their debts, and a more equally flourishing human future.

References

Alexander, M. (2010). *The new Jim Crow: Mass incarceration in the age of colorblindness.* New York, NY: New Press.

Bakeman, J. (2014, February 18). Republicans rally against Cuomo's prison-college plan. *Capital New York.* Retrieved from. http://www.capitalnewyork.com/article/albany/2014/02/8540470/republicans-rally-against-cuomos-prison-college-plan

Chang, C. (2012, July 29). Many doctors treating state's prisoners have disciplinary records themselves. *The Times-Picayune.* Retrieved from http://www.nola.com/crime/index.ssf/2012/07/many_doctors_treating_states_p.html

Christian, S. (2009, March). *Children of incarcerated parents.* National Conference of State Legislatures. Retrieved from http://www.ncsl.org/documents/cyf/childrenofincarceratedparents.pdf

Cooper, A. D., Durose, M. R., & Snyder, H. N. (2014, April 22). *Recidivism of prisoners released in 30 states in 2005: Patterns from 2005 to 2010* (NCJ 244205). Bureau of Justice Statistics. Retrieved from http://www.bjs.gov/index.cfm?ty=pbdetail&iid=4986

Davis, L. M., Bozick, R., Steele, J. L., Saunders, J., & Miles, J. N. V. (2013). *Evaluating the effectiveness of correctional education: A meta-analysis of programs that provide education to incarcerated adults.* The Rand Corporation and the U.S. Bureau of Justice Assistance. Retrieved from http://www.rand.org/pubs/research_reports/RR266.html

Directorate of Norwegian Criminal Service. (n.d.). Retrieved from http://www.kriminalomsorgen.no/english.293899.en.html

Espenshade, T. J. (2013, May 13). Growing elitism. *The Chronicle of Higher Education.* Retrieved from http://chronicle.com/article/Growing-Elitism/132641/

Henrichson, C., & Delaney, R. (2012). *The price of prisons: What incarceration costs taxpayers.* The Vera Institute. Retrieved from http://www.vera.org/sites/default/files/resources/downloads/Price_of_Prisons_updated_version_072512.pdf

New Directions for Community Colleges • DOI: 10.1002/cc

Jacobson, J. (2013, February 26). Has venture philanthropy passed its peak? *Stanford Social Innovation Review*. Retrieved May 12, 2014, from, http://www.ssireview.org/blog/entry/has_venture_philanthropy_passed_its_peak

Knafo, S. (2013, September 17). When it comes to illegal drug use, White America does the crime, Black America gets the time. *The Huffington Post*. Retrieved from http://www.huffingtonpost.com/2013/09/17/racial-disparity-drug-use_n_3941346.html

Larson, D. (2013, September 24). Why Scandinavian prisons are superior. *The Atlantic Monthly*. Retrieved from http://www.theatlantic.com/international/archive/2013/09/why-scandinavian-prisons-are-superior/279949

Minnesota Department of Corrections. (2011, November). *Effects of prison visitation on offender recidivism*. Retrieved from http://www.doc.state.mn.us/pages/files/large-files/Publications/11-11MNPrisonVisitationStudy.pdf

Page, J. (2004). *The toughest beat: Politics, punishment, and the prison officers union in California*. New York, NY: Oxford University Press.

Parke, R. D., & Clarke-Stewart, K. A. (2002, January). *From prison to home: The effect of incarceration and reentry on children, families, and communities*. U.S. Department of Health and Human Services, The Urban Institute. Retrieved from http://aspe.hhs.gov/hsp/prison2home02/parke%26stewart.pdf

Patillo, M., Weiman, D., & Western, B. (Eds.). (2004). *Imprisoning America: The social effects of mass incarceration*. New York, NY: Russell Sage.

Pratt, J. (2013). *Contrasts in punishment: An explanation of Anglophone excess and Nordic exceptionalism*. London, England: Routledge.

Reddy, V. P., & Levin, M. A. (2013, March 6). The conservative case against more prisons. *The American Conservative*. Retrieved from http://www.theamericanconservative.com/articles/the-conservative-case-against-more-prisons

Republicans criticize Cuomo proposal for state to cover inmates' college costs. (2014, February 20). *The Buffalo News*, p. C10.

Schirmer, S., Ashley, N., & Marc, M. (2009, February). *Incarcerated parents and their children: Trends 1991–2007*. The Sentencing Project. Retrieved from http://www.sentencingproject.org/doc/publications/publications/inc_incarceratedparents.pdf

Schmitt, J., Warner, K., & Gupta, S. (2010, June). *The high budgetary cost of incarceration*. The Center for Economic and Policy Research. Retrieved from http://www.cepr.net/documents/publications/incarceration-2010-06.pdf

Venture philanthropy. (2013, November 5). Retrieved from http://en.wikipedia.org/wiki/Venture_philanthropy

Wacquant, L. (2000). The new peculiar institution: On the prison as surrogate ghetto. *Theoretical Criminology*, 4(3), 377–389.

Wacquant, L. (2009). *Punishing the poor: The neoliberal government of social insecurity*. Durham, NC: Duke University Press.

Walmsley, R. (2011, May). *World prison population list*. International Centre for Prison Studies. Retrieved from http://www.prisonstudies.org/sites/prisonstudies.org/files/resources/downloads/wppl_9.pdf

Western, B. (2006). *Punishment and inequality in America*. New York, NY: Russell Sage.

Woodhouse, K. (2012, October 25). Enrollment trends: Out-of-state students form 42.6 percent of University of Michigan's freshman class. *The Ann Arbor Post*. Retrieved from http://www.annarbor.com/news/university-of-michigan-sees-increase-in-out-of-state-students/

DORAN LARSON *is a professor of English and creative writing at Hamilton College, editor of* Fourth City: Essays from the Prison in America, *and the principal investigator for The American Prison Writing Archive, a Hamilton Digital Humanities Initiative project supported by the Andrew Mellon Foundation.*

2

This chapter describes a specific initiative to offer a college program within the Oregon Department of Corrections, with a focus on the interpersonal and interinstitutional relationships needed to build such programs.

College Inside: A Case Study of the Design and Implementation of a Successful Prison College Program

Betsy Simpkins

This essay is written to share lessons learned while developing College Inside, a program of Chemeketa Community College in the Oregon Department of Corrections. Oregon currently houses 14,664 inmates in 14 prisons (Oregon Department of Corrections, 2013). There are many more on parole or postprison supervision. With an average of 427 new intakes and 377 releases every month, it is no wonder the correctional system is often described as a revolving door. Issues such as high school dropout rate, poverty, changes in legislation, drug addiction, and mandatory minimum sentencing all affect the number of Oregonians incarcerated.

Although most states face similar difficulties, Oregon has taken proactive measures to address these issues. Oregon is considered a national leader in efforts to reduce the rate of reincarceration of offenders on new criminal convictions. Through a combination of legislation and community efforts, the state has seen a 32% drop in recidivism since the early 1990s (Pew Center on the States, 2011). However, the current rate is still alarmingly high at 25.5% (Oregon Department of Corrections, 2013). These new criminal offenses are costly, impact the safety of our communities, and illustrate the ineffectiveness of current programming in the prison system.

At Chemeketa Community College, we believe that local colleges have an obligation and are uniquely positioned to impact both the rate of incarceration and recidivism. Communities have partnered with local schools, the sheriff's office, and county administrators to create innovative programs. In Marion County, for example, the combined efforts of the county and Chemeketa have resulted in a lowered recidivism rate of 17% due to a

NEW DIRECTIONS FOR COMMUNITY COLLEGES, no. 170, Summer 2015 © 2015 Wiley Periodicals, Inc.
Published online in Wiley Online Library (wileyonlinelibrary.com) • DOI: 10.1002/cc.20140

postprison alcohol and drug recovery program that also focuses on employment and education.

In 1991, Chemeketa entered into a contract with the Oregon Department of Corrections (DOC) to teach adult basic education and GED courses in Willamette Valley area prisons. Having had a presence in the prison system for 23 years, Chemeketa is committed to providing opportunities for incarcerated students. Even in the harsh environment of prison, a community college can make a difference. For Chemeketa, expanding our presence to include college degrees was a natural next step. Our program is known as College Inside.

Creating and conducting a college program inside a prison come with many challenges. But there are also many supporters who champion the importance of education as a means to ending the revolving door of incarceration. It is their efforts, in spite of the challenges, that make it possible for programs like College Inside to exist and even thrive in today's era of mass incarceration.

This essay will describe the creation and implementation of Chemeketa's College Inside program, including the justification for such programs, evaluation of success, general program design, curriculum choices, selection of students, funding, and of course, working with the DOC. The goal of this essay is to use College Inside as a roadmap to inform college administrators on the importance of this work, detail implementation of such programs, and encourage increased involvement within correctional environments nationwide.

Justifying Community College Involvement in Prison Education

Community colleges get involved with prison education for a variety of reasons. Chemeketa's decision was partly based on the acknowledgment that incarcerated students are an underserved population. The culture and mission of Chemeketa is rooted in the concept of community, and making communities safer by investing in the education of their citizens is a great example of putting the core values of the college to work. Colleges may be able to provide resources such as volunteers, instructors, community partners, and other funding in ways that strained state agencies may not. College Inside is funded entirely through private donations. There is no corporate sponsorship, no federal or state grant, and no monetary support from the DOC. It is the relationship that the college has with the community that drives this program.

Since College Inside's inception in 2007, hundreds of incarcerated people have joined in order to acquire more education. The original proposal came from two incarcerated students and turned into one class whose nine students each paid the standard, full tuition for a three-credit class, which was $261 at the time. This grew into a full two-year program for 40 students inside two prisons, later expanding to three prisons with proposals for even more degree options. To date, College Inside has served more than 350 students. The program provides opportunities for students to expand their beliefs about their abilities and future goals. This leads to positive changes that result in graduation, employment, enrollment in universities, and most importantly increased safety. These are the key justifications for prison education programs.

Is College Inside Effective?

Success of a college program in prison can be defined in many ways. Minimally, success means that students leave prison with more knowledge and sense of purpose than they came in with. We know that the transformation made possible through education has lasting effects. Our graduates are getting jobs, owning businesses, enrolling in universities, and supporting their families. Such successes are important for building a qualitative case for this work, but statistical information is an equally valid and important measure of effectiveness. Data on the number of students served, degrees awarded, postrelease activities, and how many have returned to prison can indicate the impact of the program on society.

College Inside has had 108 graduates, 53 of whom have been released. Among the graduates, the program has actually awarded 140 degrees because many pursue multiple degrees. Of the 53 graduates who have been released from prison, 41 are currently working and/or attending school (77.4%). Only two of the 53 have returned to prison, bringing the rate of recidivism to 3.8%—far below the state average. This low recidivism rate has many benefits. According to the DOC, it costs $87.08 per day to house an inmate in a correctional facility (Oregon Department of Corrections, 2013). This figure does not account for the high cost of investigation, arrest, prosecution, and certainly does not include the immeasurable emotional costs for new victims. The dollars not spent on investigating and prosecuting these new crimes can surely be invested in other programs or needed services, such as education and alcohol/drug treatment programs. In addition, by staying out of prison, these former offenders are working and contributing to the economy.

Although this low recidivism rate and the reduced costs associated with it cannot be attributed solely to College Inside, it is programs like ours that allow these fathers, sons, and brothers to go home in a more stable place emotionally, with practical skills, education, and most importantly a desire to be better men. Most of our graduates report that their experience as a college student while incarcerated was the most pivotal change that contributed to the success they now enjoy on the outside. This is the true measure of success for any prison education program.

Sustainability of programming depends on the availability of funding. There is a direct correlation between the number of students in college and the resources needed to enroll them. There is a significant lack of opportunity for personal growth and professional development in the prison system, though many incarcerated adults yearn for a chance to do something different with their lives. With sufficient funding, the interest level rises and creates a more stable, consistent student body, which is necessary for long-term sustainability.

The design of effective programs like College Inside is not without challenges. Issues regarding funding, student populations, applicable courses of study, and working with the DOC must all be addressed in order to successfully propose and implement a program.

Designing College Inside

Designing a degree program for a correctional setting requires dedication, defined goals, and a great deal of flexibility. Not every prison is interested in higher education for inmates. Since the virtual disappearance of prison programs in 1994 when federal Pell grant eligibility was eliminated for inmates, many prisons have officers on staff who were not even born when college classes were abundant in prisons throughout the 1980s and early 1990s. Therefore, it is important that any administrator contemplating a college program be aware of the need to sell the idea as a benefit to the institution.

Dedication and commitment to a program idea are essential because it may not be received enthusiastically by prison officials; even if it is welcomed, that may not translate into smooth sailing in the day-to-day operation. With College Inside, despite having support from the director, assistant director, and some superintendents (formerly called wardens), we often have difficulties with security staff and management with regard to educational practices and materials. Even after seven years, we often have to justify the purpose of our program.

Having clearly defined goals can help. For most colleges, completion of a degree or certificate program is the objective. The key is to clearly state the goal, how it benefits society, and perhaps more importantly, how it contributes to the success of the specific institution.

A reduction in the rates of recidivism and/or return to prison is one of the main objectives for College Inside. As Colette Peters, the director of the DOC, said recently, "The higher an individual's education level, the less likely they are to recidivate" (Peters, 2013). She went on to state that although the Oregon recidivism rate at the time was 26.5%, the number drops to 14% with an associate's degree (Peters, 2013). Therefore, we are confident that there is a statistical advantage for those students actually completing the degree versus those who simply participate.

For College Inside, we established guidelines for participation in the program that ensure completion of the degree prior to release. An effective college program design begins by identifying potential students, a curriculum that best suits the environment, and funding sources, as well as working with the DOC.

Choosing and Retaining Students

With limited funding, Chemeketa found it impossible to serve all of the nearly 3,000 adults incarcerated in the institutions where the college already had a presence. Therefore, selection criteria were established with the assistance of prison administrators, the donors, and college staff.

Some programs do not put restrictions on inmate participation including offense, length of sentence, release date, prison conduct, or financial means. However, College Inside implemented certain criteria. In our program, the associate's degree takes three years to complete. Therefore, we chose to focus on students with three to five years to release. This allowed students time to finish and allowed us to include more of the population than if we had only focused on students with three years left. However, as we have learned over the years, it is important to be aware of the changing population that the program will serve. At one of our facilities, it has been difficult to consistently enroll enough students with less than five years to release to fill classes and maintain a sustainable student body. We have since increased our sentence length to include those with seven years or even more in some cases.

Additionally, we require students to have 18 months of good conduct (no disciplinary problems). This serves as an incentive for inmates to maintain good conduct, and assures security personnel that we are not rewarding bad behavior. Furthermore, we require that students maintain a B average for the year.

Finally, we believe it is very important that students contribute to the cost of their own education. College Inside is a donor-funded program, but students feel more independent when they contribute. By sacrificing the few dollars they earn in prison and putting that money toward their education, students feel involved and more responsible for their success. Students pay a reasonable fee of $30 per class, which is affordable for most and helps reduce the cost of the program.

Some prison programs eliminate students with certain offenses, typically sexual offenses, but College Inside does not discriminate based on this factor. The hierarchy of prison is often based on this; however, we encourage our students to work past the labeling and judgment that surrounds them everywhere else in prison. By discouraging such behaviors, we have greatly reduced the self-segregation that occurs based on race, criminal offense, or sexual orientation. Many of our students say that prior to joining the program, they would never have talked to "that" person, or that they "used" to feel a certain way about "those" people. But after a while in the college program, they realize that they can work together with people who

NEW DIRECTIONS FOR COMMUNITY COLLEGES • DOI: 10.1002/cc

are different from them, regardless of prison politics. We expect them to rise above, and so they do.

Keeping a student in a program is almost as important as getting them to join in the first place. It is rare that an incarcerated student will gather enough courage and money to join only to drop out later. But even these rare drops may be anticipated and prevented. Many incarcerated students have not had positive educational experiences in traditional classroom settings. Providing college readiness classes, including developmental math and writing courses and study skills classes, can help provide a foundation that may reduce the chance the student will get overwhelmed and simply quit.

Another way to prevent dropouts is to work with the student to define his interest in college, what he hopes to accomplish, and whether or not he is prepared for the work necessary to achieve that goal. Taking the time to connect with a student about his experience helps identify areas where the student could use additional assistance, or provides an opportunity for encouragement and positive reinforcement. This helps the student feel confident, cared about, and secure in his choices, all of which lead to retaining that student. Based on Chemeketa's student records, these strategies have helped lead College Inside to retain 86.7% of eligible, degree-seeking students in the program. Furthermore, 79.1% of eligible, degree-seeking students have successfully graduated from the program since its inception in 2007. This success is due to clear standards for selecting students and utilizing resources to build strong educational foundations and support throughout their academic careers.

Curriculum: Choosing a Degree Path

Although some students intend to pursue a four-year degree once released from prison, most are undecided about their prospective major/career when they are released. Therefore, Chemeketa provides a variety of studies that are likely to impact the most students. We offer liberal arts and business transfer degrees. We also oversee an automotive technician degree program and a one-year computer-aided design (CAD) certification program. This combination of vocational and academic studies offers a wide array of options to prepare students for life after prison.

There are challenges that come with selecting degree programs. We would love to offer computer programming, graphic design, or counseling degrees, but these are difficult due to limitations that come with prison. For example, in the Oregon adult prison system, there is no Internet access for inmates. This makes it nearly impossible to offer courses that require a great deal of research, practicums, or web-based material.

To choose the right curriculum, it is important to be familiar with the institution policies, the inmate population, and the workforce needs in the local community. With this information, any college will surely be able to find suitable programs of study to produce successful and employable graduates.

Funding: Paying for College Inside

Funding for the College Inside program has come from various sources. Initially the students paid full tuition. Then, in late 2007, Chemeketa was contacted by a local businessman interested in funding a program in an effort to effect more of a change than current prison programs. His quarterly donations allowed us to create our original program. Without this benefactor, the College Inside program could not exist in its current form. Although we did not seek out such sponsorship, we garnered his continued support through our demonstrated successes. By providing quarterly progress reports with data such as the outstanding GPAs of our students and the increase in student participation, we were able to consistently prove that the donated money was put to excellent use, and there was a good return on the investment.

We used this support and our proven achievements as a basis for additional funding requests. In 2011, Chemeketa received a federal grant to provide higher education to youth offenders. The infrastructure we had in place made us very competitive and we secured the funding for 1.5 years until the federal money was exhausted.

Losing funding is common in prison programs. If there were one piece of advice I would give to any administrator contemplating a prison education program, it would be to make funding a top priority. This can be difficult and time consuming. However, relying on only one source of funding may result in donation exhaustion. This is what happened to College Inside in 2013, when our main donor decided that, although he believed in our mission and was impressed with our progress, he had funded the program long enough. For us, this loss was devastating. But it created an opportunity to focus on finding other support. As a result, we applied for and received funding from other sources, including a private nonprofit organization. This funding is allowing us to continue our work through 2015 and ensure another 18 graduates.

But in an effort to diversify our funding even more, we chose to see this as a chance to get creative with our own college. Dedicated staff on campus are assisting with marketing and grant writing specifically for College Inside. To date, this has resulted in approximately $16,500 in donations from the community. In addition, the administration has allowed full-time faculty to teach a class for us as part of their regular schedule. This is a creative way to allow us access to instructors who want to teach in the prison program, but in a way that minimizes costs to our program. Another solution that has consistently helped is that the college agreed to charge only the cost to cover the instructor salary, rather than full tuition from each student. This enables us to maximize the number of students we can serve for the same cost.

Funding for education programs in prison is very difficult. There may be political ramifications for corporations who choose to support prison college programs, and public support requires a great deal of open communication and presence in the community. However, with the help of the college, demonstrable successes, and considerable efforts to find funding, I am confident that College Inside will carry on and can serve as a wonderful example to any college attempting the same.

Working With the DOC

To work effectively with the DOC, it is important to understand what the agency is and how it operates. Walking into a prison can feel like stepping over a threshold into another world. It is a true test of patience, with the seemingly constant wait for doors to slide open and slam shut, the showing of ID, and a heightened sense of awareness of eyes from staff and inmates all around. There is a myriad of reactions to the presence of nonsecurity staff, including smiles, sneers, or more commonly a complete lack of acknowledgment at all. The daily choice to walk into a prison to teach is a testament to the advocates who do this work.

The DOC is a paramilitary organization with increasing ranks and responsibilities. It is a state agency headed by an appointed director with several levels of management. Originally designed to rehabilitate offenders, prisons are now considered by most to be warehouses where people are "stored" until released back into society. Overcrowding, budget constraints, and antiquated ideology create an environment where hostility, selfishness, and sadness abound. The struggle for power and control between officers charged with maintaining order and inmates striving to retain or create a sense of self is exacerbated by a lack of education, self-esteem, and mutual respect.

Correctional administrators and officers have a tremendous responsibility to communities, victims, and inmates themselves. Perhaps prisons are necessary evils of our society. However, many policies adopted by the DOC in order to protect inmates and staff seem to have the opposite effect. Mandates to refer to inmates only by their last name, extreme sensitivity to staff developing any sort of positive relationship with inmates, and the generally accepted practice of demeaning and disrespectful treatment of inmates and staff all contribute to an overall sense of distrust and animosity. I suggest that there is a fundamental flaw in this system, which is the overt prohibition of simple humanity. It is a lack of humanity and empathy that allowed these offenders to commit the crimes for which they are in prison. It appears as if our prisons are designed not to change that, but rather, to knowingly encourage it through the modeling of negative behavior, lack of counseling or self-improvement opportunities, and general staff sentiment. Does it have to be this way?

NEW DIRECTIONS FOR COMMUNITY COLLEGES • DOI: 10.1002/cc

Some institutions have embraced their stated mission of rehabilitation through proper example and role modeling. For instance, in one prison, the support for College Inside is apparent from the superintendent down to the lowest-ranking officer. The management team opened the floor one additional day per week to accommodate our college schedule. In preparation for our graduation ceremony, I was told on multiple occasions to simply ask for what I needed and they would see to it. They have allowed security staff to supervise our weekend study hall sessions when our staff is not available. It is rare that I hear stories from our students about officers targeting them or making negative remarks about their pursuit of higher education. And finally, when inappropriate behavior does occur, whether to staff or inmates, it is handled quickly and with respect for us as educators.

In contrast, another facility only five miles away from the first seems to epitomize all that is negative and stereotypical of prison. When presented with further educational opportunities at no cost to the institution, the superintendent simply said "no." Officers routinely ignore staff or, sometimes worse, engage in verbal altercations because of sheer animosity for the program. The last few graduation ceremonies have been disastrous, with disrespectful treatment of students and guests and preparations being completely ignored by security. Students report on a daily basis that certain officers harass and threaten them simply because they are in college. Many feel so on edge due to this treatment that they hope we start a college program at another facility so they can simply transfer to get away. Complaints from students as well as staff go unanswered, or we are told that somebody will "talk to" the certain officer. The code of silence is very strong in facilities like this, where there is very little incentive to report bad behavior and the administration seems unable or unwilling to force improvements. In this facility, education is not seen as a benefit, but rather an inconvenience that inhibits an officer's ability to manage the "warehouse" as he sees fit.

Managing a college program in an environment such as this is challenging to say the least. However, the benefits of establishing and maintaining a positive relationship with the DOC are immense and are therefore worth the effort. If the DOC can share in the mission to educate the population, then the students feel supported, the instructors and the college feel like partners with the DOC, and in general it makes for a much nicer place to live and work. So it is essential that college representatives try to create this partnership early. To this end, it is helpful to gather all the necessary stakeholders, DOC leadership, and specific prison officials and allow them to be involved with the project from the beginning.

Although this partnership with DOC is vital to the success of any college program, it cannot come at the expense of staff and students. Often the culture of a prison, a change in administration, or simply a particular officer can derail an entire program. Instructors, students, and college administrators should not be required to endure disrespect, mistreatment, or

threatening behavior from inmates, correctional staff, or even prison officials. Discussions with the DOC should be frank regarding this topic. We
have learned that enduring such treatment, based on a belief that the benefit to the students will outweigh the negatives that come from such harass-
ment, leads to unhappy workplaces, dissatisfied staff, and fearful students.
Very little positive can come from this and it would be wiser to seek a more
appropriate environment for the program.

Of course a big part of the success of College Inside has been the salesmanship. We must all remember that officers, administrators, and other
contractors working in prison do not always know what we do or agree
with why we do it. Knowing the facts of the program can help. Everybody
participating in the college program should be able to answer the following
questions. Why should inmates get a college education? How does this program help anybody? What about the victims, what do they deserve? And
finally, why is it worth spending any money at all on programs like this?

As the facts of the program filter through the various layers of DOC,
the agency and the individual prisons begin to change. The partnership
that is created through the shared vision of reducing recidivism and creating safer communities is what allows for and motivates improvement in
our correctional system. Working with DOC can be a roller coaster ride of
inconsistencies, negativity, and punitive ideologies. But, through positive
salesmanship, demonstrable successes, and respect for the work of security
staff, we can create allies and become true partners within DOC.

Conclusion

The involvement of a community college in prison education has many
advantages to both institutions. Colleges often have a mission to serve a
variety of nontraditional students. The community college is dedicated to
addressing the educational needs of underserved populations, so they are
more likely to be able to secure grants and are generally more connected
with communities than is a state agency like the DOC. Community colleges are simply the most logical and best situated institutions to provide
higher learning in a prison setting.

As discussed, designing and implementing a college program in a
prison may not be the easiest undertaking. It requires funding, identifying
programs of study, eligible students, outcome objectives, and finding ways
to establish positive working relationships with the DOC. Even though College Inside should be considered a success, Chemeketa learned some of
these lessons the hard way.

Having identified many reasons why a college might invest in a prison
education program, many may still find it a very difficult decision whether
or not they should get involved in this work. Simply put, I think the answer
is yes. Were it not for the interest, infrastructure, and support of Chemeketa
Community College, all the benefits that Oregon has seen in the last seven

years as a result of College Inside would be nonexistent. The involvement of the college in the prisons has led to increased safety and stability both inside and outside of the prison and provided much-needed motivation for future education to incarcerated men in Oregon. This translates into fewer men returning to prison, more fathers parenting their kids, and in the end, much safer cities.

The challenges with prison education are many, from the revolving door of incarceration, to the lack of college readiness, to dealing with the difficulties of prison operations. However, the gifts are even greater and culminate in a truly transformative experience. I am reminded of one of our graduates, who was released from prison only to courageously return as an invited guest speaker. Every graduation I witness the many men who can, at last, look their children or parents in the eye and feel they deserve the love shining back at them. These men are changed, and that is the result of community college involvement in prison education.

As community colleges around the country contemplate programs that can significantly impact their local communities, I encourage administrators to consider the many benefits of prison education, and specifically college programs like College Inside. If we as a society truly want to end this epidemic of incarceration in America, we must act. Education is the best place to start.

References

Oregon Department of Corrections. (2013, June). DOC quick facts. *Issue Brief, 53.* Retrieved August 13, 2014, from http://www.oregon.gov/doc/GECO/docs/pdf/IB_53 _Quick_Facts_06_14.pdf

Peters, C. (2013, July 26). Commencement speech. Keynote Speech at Chemeketa Community College Graduation Ceremony, Salem, OR.

Pew Center on the States. (2011, April). *State of recidivism: The revolving door of America's prisons.* Washington, DC: The Pew Charitable Trusts.

BETSY SIMPKINS, MA.ED, is the program coordinator for College Inside, an associate's degree-granting program in Oregon state prisons operated by Chemeketa Community College.

NEW DIRECTIONS FOR COMMUNITY COLLEGES • DOI: 10.1002/cc

3

Three authors describe a collaboration between a Massachusetts college and a nearby prison, which leveraged the volunteer efforts of a college professor by including incarcerated men who assisted in Spanish language teaching inside and outside the classroom.

Community Colleges and Spanish Language Instruction: Peer Pedagogy in Prison

Jenifer D. Drew, José Duval, James R. Cyr

This paper provides a description of a Spanish language curriculum, part of a prison postsecondary education program, offered by a four-year institution inside a state prison. This curriculum is well-suited to become part of prison education offered by community colleges, in that the four-semester format is compatible with the two-year structure, and is responsive to the mission of the community college. In a nation in which Spanish speakers comprise an increasing proportion of the population, the economic and social benefits of bilingualism are both practical and profound. Four semesters of language while incarcerated allows graduates to add "working knowledge of Spanish" to their job applications when they are released and significantly enhances their opportunities for employment. From the point of view of rehabilitation and reentry, education while incarcerated mitigates the stigma of incarceration and enhances the perception of former prisoners in the eyes of the community (Pew Center on the States, 2009). Finally, when the formerly incarcerated are released to return home and find work, the benefits of prison postsecondary education extend to the students' families and communities.

This curriculum involves native-speaking prisoners, who serve as unpaid teaching assistants (TAs) under the supervision of one professor from the sponsoring entity or educational institution. The curriculum offers the benefits of small-group instruction, exposure to natural accents, and an economy of scale for the college. There is a collateral benefit important to those who teach in prisons: that postsecondary education, particularly liberal arts education, has the ability to effect a permanent and profound

New Directions for Community Colleges, no. 170, Summer 2015 © 2015 Wiley Periodicals, Inc.
Published online in Wiley Online Library (wileyonlinelibrary.com) • DOI: 10.1002/cc.20141

change in the "cognitive landscape" of students (Sampson & Wilson, 1990). This restorative quality of prison education is magnified when incarcerated students learn through peer instruction, as they witness fellow prisoners entrusted by an outside academic institution to become educators.

The prison environment is tightly controlled, concerned with security and predictability. For this reason, the implementation of a college program in a correctional setting differs in specific ways from implementation of such a program on campus. In the decade since initial implementation of this peer-instructed language program, more than 100 incarcerated students have completed the four semesters of Spanish language curriculum. This paper describes the challenges, the specific structural and cultural obstacles encountered at implementation, as well as some effective responses to those challenges learned over 10 years and five cohorts. It is hoped the authors' experience will be useful to those who would offer their own peer-taught language program in a correctional setting. The insights shared in this paper are applicable to any such program in a correctional setting; for that matter, many extend beyond language instruction and are generalizable to prison postsecondary educational as a whole.

The Selection and Training of Incarcerated Teaching Assistants

This project began when students enrolled in a prison education program asked for a formal course in Spanish. Efforts at conversational Spanish were happening informally in the living units at the prison, but in the absence of printed texts and a classroom structure, they were short-lived. Students recognized that a facility in Spanish would be of value, socially and vocationally. It was determined that a minimum of four semesters were needed to achieve, if not fluency, at least the "working knowledge" the students wished to acquire.

The first question was who would teach the curriculum. The search for a professor who would be new to the prison program but willing to commit to four semesters proved unsuccessful. However, many incarcerated men who had graduated from the program were native Spanish speakers. We decided that with preparation, supervision, and a good textbook, they could serve as TAs, while a faculty member from outside provided guidance and supervision. It was resolved that, while the TAs would be charged with instruction, a professor, who spoke beginning-level Spanish, would be in the classroom at all times and would meet with TAs before, during, and after each semester to guide their teaching. Furthermore, prior to entering the classroom, TAs would undergo a course in pedagogy with that professor, study the textbook, and be instructed in the philosophy of teaching, the mechanics of syllabus construction, lesson planning, and student learning styles.

Four incarcerated graduates of the program were selected to serve as TAs: one Dominican, one Columbian, and two Puerto Ricans. This chapter is authored by two of the TAs and the professor who facilitated the program. The comments quoted in the remainder of this essay are taken from the TAs' journal entries or other students' responses to requests to provide course feedback. The four-semester curriculum has been repeated with five cohorts, and is about to begin with a sixth.

There is an informal code of conduct enforced by people incarcerated at the prison that is very clear on matters of ethics, trustworthiness, and loyalty to one's peers. An awareness of this code is crucial for successful program implementation. As one TA reflected in his teaching journal,

> In an environment like prison the boundaries between "solid con" and "rat" or informant are precarious at best. The stigma of that label is evident in that men often will go out of their way not to have too much contact with authority figures, like the guards, the administration, etc. Individuals feel hesitant to assume a position which can be viewed as "acting like a cop," since this equates with being labeled a snitch or rat. So it was with much trepidation that we assumed the role of educator/TA and the mantle of authority that this role brought with it. At no moment did we want to be perceived as being or acting like "cops." We hazarded our reputations in the belief that what we were doing would be momentous and at the same time offer a little of ourselves and our cultures to the students.

Peer Language Instruction in Prison: Challenges

Our first challenge was to confront the fact that the prison language program, unlike most language programs, would not be supported by a language lab. On campus, language classes meet daily and/or require attendance at a language lab or proof of completion of online interactive modules. In the state in which this program operates, prisoners do not have access to electronics, yet the need to hear the same phrase over and over is central to language acquisition.

Responding to the absence of a language lab, we persuaded prison authorities to allow students to borrow compact disc (CD) players from the school in order to listen to language CDs in their cells. We also required Spanish television; students watched *telenovelas* in Spanish and discussed them in class. As students became engaged with the characters and plots of Spanish-language television, discussions grew heated among students determined to make their point, despite having to use their limited Spanish to do so. A fourth-semester student who was also a musician described how he tried out his language skills after his band performed at a prisoner-run group for native speakers:

> After my band was introduced, and we began the first song, I said, *"Como estan muchachos? Estan listos para escuchar musica rock?"* and later... *"Oye! Dime si han escuchando algo como esto?!"* (How are you, guys? Are you ready

to listen to some rock and roll? Hey, tell me if you've ever heard anything like this?!) This took the entire audience by surprise, and they gave a loud cheer in response. Since the show, I have been approached and congratulated by Whites, Blacks, Asians, and Hispanics.

It was challenging to find a language teacher willing to make a four-semester commitment to a prison program. We decided that four semesters would be necessary to achieve a "working knowledge" of Spanish. A four-semester curriculum permits the completion of a comprehensive text, reading and analysis of Spanish prose and poetry, and one entire semester of total conversational immersion.

As mentioned earlier, the program trained Spanish-speaking prisoners to serve as TAs. By excluding prisoners with less than two years before parole eligibility, it was ensured that the TAs would be there for the duration. The program began with four TAs in the first semester, but allowed for their departure when necessary. For example one TA left to attend to his upcoming appeal, and another had to stop because the demands of his prison job made it difficult to do his share. Over three semesters, we lost 11 of the original 26 students, and two of the four original TAs. Four instructors would have been more than were needed and the two remaining TAs managed the class of 15 handily.

The program experienced difficulty with the lack of control over interaction, contact hours, and scheduling. A lockdown could cancel an entire week of instruction, for instance. Prison teachers were forced to accept that the first concern in prison is security rather than education. Long breaks between semesters, especially if no summer classes are offered, interfered with the continuity of the pedagogy. TAs and the supervising professor must find creative ways to avoid the loss of language skills during breaks.

We responded by developing a curricular sequence that was not attached to specific dates, and we adopted a stance of flexibility with respect to the need for make-up classes. We routinely gave our students assignments during vacations, holidays, and summer recess. These assignments were expected to be completed at the first meeting after break, a practice students on campus would never abide, but was welcomed by prison students.

We needed to respond to the lack of traditional office hours in the prison program. While there are many Spanish-speaking people in their units, not all Latino prisoners are conversant with the Spanish grammar students learn in class. Consequently, students routinely stopped the TAs in the yard, in the chow line, or in the gym and asked for clarification. While the TAs were gratified by the interest, we were concerned that they would have no time available to work on their other projects, and that they would not be uniformly available to all students. To help the TAs structure the demands on their time, and allow for one-on-one help with struggling students, the program established fixed office hours with the TAs three times a week, in the prison library. The supervising professor asked the students to confine their questions to office hours, and in the main they did.

Supervision of the TAs was challenging to the professor and TAs alike. It can be very difficult to provide TAs with adequate guidance, and still stay out of their way as they learn to teach and gain confidence. On campus, TAs and the supervising professor would do a lot of communicating about the course and the students' progress. Much would be hashed out and decided in informal meetings. This was not possible because the class occurred during the only three hours weekly the faculty member was in the prison. During class, the supervising professor watched TAs teach, but had little time to offer thoughtful and immediate feedback; communication was pointed and rushed. Equally challenging were the efforts of the TAs to work as a team and trust themselves to construct lesson plans in the supervising professor's absence.

To respond to these potential deficits, each TA was given a notebook. As each took his turn at teaching, the supervising professor made notes in his notebook and handed his notebook back to him, to be read later. Sometimes, the professor asked the TA questions in the notebook, and received his answers during the following class. Sometimes, when a TA had general questions about teaching, his questions were answered in depth by the professor in the notebook in such a way that it could be shared by all of the TAs. Ultimately, the supervising professor had to trust the TAs, who had to learn to trust themselves as they are left to improvise between visits from the professor.

The ability of the TAs to work as a team came gradually, a function of TAs preparing before they entered the classroom, becoming aware of their abilities, and realizing the trust that the supervising professor placed in them. Most often, one TA would propose a plan, they would work together to institute it, meet and assess it later, with the supervising professor's input. In other words, they would learn by doing—as most new teachers do.

To further bolster their confidence, the program invited Spanish professors from campus to visit the prison and teach a master class. The professors watched the TAs teach, then modeled techniques for the TAs who incorporated these new techniques into their teaching. This was inspirational for the TAs, and increased their confidence in their abilities. Since many decisions were left to the judgment and creativity of the TAs in the absence of any professor, it was vital that TAs felt empowered to make heuristic decisions as needed. As one TA shared,

When it came time to take the reins of the class or to make decisions without the permission of the professor, some felt we had to check first, and others of us felt we did not have to seek express [sic] permission from the professor for every minor detail and nuance that occurred in the classroom.

I think this hesitancy and lack of self-assurance showed and it was evident in our dealings with each other, maybe not so much to the professor, but to the students, who recognized the situation.

It can be extremely challenging to manage discrepancy and inconsistency in peer education, especially in prison when TAs are fellow prisoners (Jackson & Burke, 1965). A correctional setting is a fragile environment in terms of respect and relative strata, of power and authority. What follows are several examples of challenges faced by the supervising professor, who, learning by trial and error, came to understand the challenges of managing status in a peer-instructed prison classroom.

First, the professor naïvely assumed the TAs could easily exercise authority over their peers. Only later did it become apparent the finesse required of TAs to maintain their positions as "solid cons," while wielding the power and authority the professor had granted them. This was mentioned earlier: the TAs had to deal with the expectations of fellow prisoners that they would "stick together" and use their access to course material to aid their peers.

Another challenge stemmed from one of the great advantages of learning Spanish in prison: the opportunity for students to speak Spanish with native speakers in their housing units. The supervising professor thought it was an advantage, but enrolled students came to realize that sometimes native speakers speak informally, sprinkling their language with "Spanglish" and grammatical errors. Students enrolled in the Spanish class could not correct their grammar without running the risk of insulting them. It would have been useful for the supervising professor to help students prepare for those interactions.

Given that many of the fluent Spanish speakers at the prison had learned Spanish aurally, and thus in the dialect of their home area, there was an emergent challenge in evaluating whether dialect speakers were qualified to take third and fourth semester Spanish. One student who enrolled in the third semester reports:

> As a Dominicano, I was raised speaking a dialect of Spanish, and it's not until now that I'm beginning to grasp the grammar and context of the Spanish language ... Regardless of my ability to speak Spanish, I have been ridiculed by fellow Spanish speakers for not speaking properly—this is one of the many reasons why I'm so adamant about attending this Spanish class ... At first I was under the impression that it would be too easy for me until I began to work in the textbook over the summer. The things I've learned that I never even knew before have been of tremendous help to me already.

Another challenge related to status arose when the professor assumed that clear demarcations of elevated status—titles—would help TAs manage the status discrepancy inherent in their role. In fact the opposite was true.

New Directions for Community Colleges • DOI: 10.1002/cc

For example, it was suggested that while the supervising professor would be *Profesora*, the TAs would be *Don*, an honorific short of *Profesor* or *Maestro*, but signifying a status above *estudiante*/student. The students, meanwhile, would be given Spanish names. This suggestion only served to increase the awkwardness of the TAs' position among their peers. The students accepted the professor's suggestion of Spanish names, but as adults, wanted more say in them than they had been given. For example, members of the Nation of Islam did not want to change the names they had taken upon conversion. All this jockeying over names and titles was time consuming and ultimately unnecessary.

Another status-transgressive circumstance arose because some of the students worked harder and/or were naturally more gifted in language, thus leading to an apparent stratification of levels of skill within the class. TAs had to deal with this pedagogically, and balance differentiated treatment with the highly sensitive demands for respect that arise in prison. The professor was resistant to such a ranking of students, concerned it would be discouraging and impede their learning. Still, these divisions in skill level were apparent; they frustrated the more capable students, and inhibited the less competent students.

Peer Language Instruction in Prison: Solutions

The TAs and supervising professor found ways to respond to all these challenges by responding to their students and to the prison environment, and sometimes by abandoning more traditional pedagogy. Students brought queries about "Spanglish" to class and learned not to rely on native speakers to augment their instruction, but also never to correct them. The native speakers who had learned their language aurally joined the class in the third and fourth semesters and enhanced it with their fluency. These native speakers made what now seems an obvious point: that studying the grammatical roots of Spanish, one's native language, is akin to fluent English speakers studying the grammar of their mother tongue.

Imposing Spanish names on students and honorific titles on TAs was not useful and as soon as they could they dropped the honorifics. If Spanish names were used by students at all, it was only with levity and during immersive class presentations. The teaching assistants could teach best by maintaining their comradeship with the students, rather than accepting the stratifying offer of a title. The supervising professor made use of Spanish names optional for subsequent cohorts.

In the matter of the professor's concerns over tracking, TAs responded by proceeding gingerly to divide the class into groups that went unnamed. When handled respectfully, students appreciated being grouped by ability. As adults, they were not fooled by euphemism when groups were made distinct for in-class exercises. They embraced their groups with good humor. The more capable speakers enjoyed the smaller groups, ranging from six to ten students, as they gave them more air time to practice speaking. Meanwhile, the most reticent members of the class escaped the impatience of the others as each one took his turn in his group.

A final note on the challenge of managing status discrepancy in prison: For prison education to be as emancipatory as it can be, it is sometimes necessary for professors to check their own prejudices, ones that diminish the respect due their students (Brookfield, 1995; Freire, 1970). For example, the supervising professor suggested students think of topics around which they would like to structure their immersion discussions, and provided examples: the yard, the chow line, the gym, prison programs. These suggestions were met with a marked lack of enthusiasm, followed by an instructive class discussion. Students pointed out that prison was where they were, but not who they were. They reminded the professor that their interests were like the interests of men anywhere: sports, work, food, politics, entertainment, and families. They preferred to engage in discussions of those more meaningful topics, not the environment that surrounded them. When the professor followed their lead and abandoned prison-specific topics, discussion became so animated that students forgot their language limitations. As a TA instinctively realized:

> We need to provide them with opportunities that would enable them to develop proficiency—a lot of talking and listening in Spanish. The topics and exercises for igniting their interest should be of common interest, something contemporary. Stuff that has been on TV recently, recent topics such as violence in sports, and even topics that for the last few years have been the cause of much debate, like immigration and the death penalty. We need to address the whole man.

Conclusion

The challenges of prison education were convertible to opportunities. As we responded to these challenges, solutions evolved, given a will to serve and a determination to learn. Together, the professor, the peer TAs, and the enrolled students accomplished four important ends:

1. Enrolled students completed four semesters of demanding work with native speakers, and emerged with naturalistic accents and an appreciation for Spanish-speaking cultures.
2. TAs with college degrees but no teaching experience, together with a supervising professor, designed an intense pedagogy for peer language instruction.
3. Status discrepancy issues, which are especially pressing in prison, were overcome.
4. TAs became role models, as incarcerated students saw prisoners like themselves entrusted to be competent, ethical, and trustworthy.

The curriculum described in this paper is not only relatively inexpensive, but it makes the most of aspects of prison not necessarily found in the free world: plenty of English speakers and Spanish speakers in one place. Such a program thrived among a population determined to learn. Finally, it promoted the noncognitive skills necessary for growth—self-respect, integrity, empathy, and autonomy—that motivate educators at community colleges and every educational setting.

A language program in prison enhances employment opportunities among its graduates, as language proficiency can give released prisoners an edge in the job market. Since 2004, when the Spanish curriculum was instituted, some of these newly bilingual students have left prison and entered training programs to become community and medical interpreters. Students have left prison to use their Spanish on the job with Latino coworkers and employers. TAs have been exposed to the pleasure of serving others, in this case "giving back" through educating them.

The fragile nature of the prisoner culture can be bolstered by peer instruction. Mutual respect can be enhanced, as peer teaching is a source of pride to both students and TAs. Knowledge of one another's culture and language can increase appreciation of diverse cultures within the heterogeneous, but generally socially segregated, prison setting. Born of necessity, the curriculum can enhance the self-esteem of not only the TAs, but also the prisoner/students who see themselves in the trusted TAs. As one TA reported,

> The opportunity to teach other inmates is also of great significance from a rehabilitative point of view. The teaching assistant responds to his calling with honor and enthusiasm because he is in a place where most people think he can't be trusted or even relied upon. We TAs feel that being entrusted with such a big responsibility by an institution such as [the university] is a sign of hope when others are saying that we are worthless.

The rehabilitative and restorative properties of prison education are enhanced by peer instruction. Students learn to speak Spanish and they learn that fellow prisoners are trusted to teach them. Academics learn what community college educators already know: to respect the adult learner's need for honesty and intellectual challenge, and to see their students beyond their current circumstances. Prison students learn to accept academic norms along with prison ones, to embrace the standards dictated by the classroom as well as those dictated by the yard. This curriculum can be replicated by any community college interested in teaching in a correctional setting. As helpful as a working knowledge of Spanish may be to reentry, the learning—by community college, supervising professor, incarcerated TAs and students—goes well beyond language acquisition.

References

Brookfield, S. D. (1995). *Becoming a critically reflective teacher*. San Francisco, CA: Jossey-Bass.

Freire, P. (1970). *Pedagogy of the oppressed*. New York, NY: Herter and Herter.

Jackson, E. F., & Burke, P. J. (1965). Status and symptoms of stress: Additive and interactive effects. *American Sociological Review, 30*(4), 556–564.

Pew Center on the States. (2009, March). *One in 31: The long reach of American corrections*. Washington, DC: The Pew Charitable Trust.

Sampson, R. J., & Wilson, W. J. (1990). Toward a theory of race, crime, and urban inequality. In J. Hagan & R. D. Peterson (Eds.), *Crime and inequality* (pp. 37–54). Palo Alto, CA: Stanford University Press.

JENIFER D. DREW, PHD, *is an associate professor of justice studies and social science at Lasell College, and former director of the Boston University Prison Education Program.*

JOSÉ DUVAL *is no longer incarcerated and is enrolled in graduate school.*

JAMES R. CYR *graduated summa cum laude from the prison education program of which this curriculum is part and is active in educational affairs at the prison, where he is serving a life sentence.*

Two authors describe how teaching Spanish in an Illinois prison led them to rewrite the examples used in a Spanish textbook and engage incarcerated students in novel ways in order to make up for the lack of conventional classroom resources.

The Challenges and Rewards of Teaching Spanish in a Community College Prison Program

Erick Nava Palomino, Lee Ragsdale

Introduction, by Lee Ragsdale

In this chapter, I will describe the significant challenges to teaching Spanish in a community college prison program; I will show how collaboration with incarcerated teaching assistants enrolled in a university program along with the adaptation of typical college classroom materials made it a very productive experience that meets an unaddressed need in America's criminal justice and immigration detention systems. My coauthor, a former teaching assistant in the class I describe, will then speak about his experience in the program.

In January 2010, I began teaching the first Spanish course through the Danville Area Community College offered to incarcerated individuals at Danville Correctional Center, a men's medium security prison in east-central Illinois. I had begun as a volunteer through the only four-year university program in the state, led by the University of Illinois, Urbana-Champaign, which offered the only four-year college program for incarcerated people in the state. The University of Illinois program provides not only upper-division college courses but has a number of unique programs such as a mindfulness and meditation group, regular writing workshops, and a family and community engagement program, as well as an ESL peer tutoring program. It was in the latter program that I became involved, helping to train incarcerated University of Illinois students to become English-as-a-second-language tutors in order to meet the needs of some of the 400 plus Spanish speakers in the facility. In this capacity, I got to know those who

NEW DIRECTIONS FOR COMMUNITY COLLEGES, no. 170, Summer 2015 © 2015 Wiley Periodicals, Inc.
Published online in Wiley Online Library (wileyonlinelibrary.com) • DOI: 10.1002/cc.20142

would become teaching assistants in my class, as well as the coordinator, who was in a position to make the Spanish class a reality.

There was no job posting for a Spanish teacher at the prison, I simply approached the director and informed her that I had just completed my master's degree in Spanish linguistics and would love to offer a course at Danville. She was enthusiastic, as was the dean at the college whose approval was required, and two months later, I was teaching Spanish I with 33 students of all ages and backgrounds.

The first challenge we faced was the lack of books, since the course had never before been offered; the sister program through the University of Illinois was kind enough to provide funds to purchase 35 used textbooks primarily through Amazon.com. I chose Bill VanPatten's *¿Sabías qué?* (VanPatten, Lee, Ballman, & Farley, 2007), a standard of communicative language teaching.

The idea of communicative language teaching is that grammar, pronunciation, and vocabulary are not taught in a vacuum but rather are applied in meaningful communication to complete tasks. As a result, the book focused on the experiences of the typical college students. Mine were anything but. Activities included interviewing classmates about weekend plans whose options included going to the mall, attending a party, or going out to eat. Surveys were to be conducted on the pros and cons of apartment versus dorm living. This was my first lesson on how teaching in prison is in fact *not* like teaching on the outside.

We reworked the communicative language exercises to allow the students an opportunity to talk about authentic experiences meaningful to them. I adapted activities to fit where possible and created ones where necessary. While studying food vocabulary, instead of presenting students with a restaurant menu, which many had not seen in years, I grabbed the cafeteria menu for that week and created an information gap activity where students had to work together to compile a complete menu. Students engaged with the task and even took the opportunity to educate me about what's really served at the cafeteria, in spite of what might be indicated on the menu. "That beef stew is not meat, but soy," a student explained to me.

As a community college teacher, I had the option of reaching out to Spanish-speaking men incarcerated at the prison and enlisting them as teaching assistants. This proved invaluable to making my students' experience more meaningful. As a former volunteer at the University of Illinois program, I had worked with several incarcerated university students who were interested in becoming teachers upon release. They were bilingual, training to become tutors, and even taking linguistics courses through the University of Illinois, so they were in a perfect position to assist in class.

This "human resource" of native Spanish-speaking tutors/teaching assistants was invaluable in enriching the learning experience of students in my class, which also helped to mitigate many of the limitations inherent to teaching in a prison environment. For these particular students, the

New Directions for Community Colleges • DOI: 10.1002/cc

Spanish class was not just an abstract foreign language requirement that might as well be spent talking about campus trivia. Rather, it was the lived language of hundreds of people whom they were living with in a prison. That's where we found meaningful communication experiences that could be linked to the completion of everyday tasks. Being aware of the resource of native Spanish speakers both in the classroom and in the general population allowed me to create assignments around interacting and learning from Spanish speakers in the prison.

Differences in Teaching Language on the Outside Versus in Prison

A typical community college language course would likely have the following characteristics:

- 22–25 students per class
- Access to the Internet, public libraries, and bookstores
- An online study module component
- Out-of-class audio reinforcement (often through the online component)
- Opportunities for cultural engagement
- 16 weeks, 2–3 hours a week

My Spanish I class at Danville Correctional Center had the following characteristics:

- 30–33 students
- No Internet access, limited access to a small library with limited stocks, limited access to books (essentially, a friend or family member would have to send any books)
- No online study module component
- Out-of-class audio reinforcement in the form of optional cassette tapes or interaction with Spanish speakers
- Opportunities for cultural engagement with Spanish-speaking peers if desired
- 6 weeks, 9 hours a week

The use of native Spanish-speaking teaching assistants did much more than make up for many of these limitations; in many cases, their contribution to the classroom actually provided my students with a richer experience than they might have found in a traditional community college setting.

Using native Spanish-speaking teaching assistants in the classroom allowed me to address the large student-to-teacher ratio. The assistants often circulated around the room to answer questions, which students were often more willing to ask of a peer than an instructor. We also regularly divided up into small groups with one teaching assistant in each to guide the activity, therefore essentially shrinking the size of the learning community, if only for 10–15 minutes.

The teaching assistants also helped grow the quantity of teaching to match the large class size. Having a high number of students that met frequently would have meant many fewer homework assignments were it not for the teaching assistants who often took on the task of grading and providing meaningful feedback to the students. A few teaching assistants even took on the role of tutoring students with special needs and administering exams for students who needed extended time. In these ways, the large class size was addressed by essentially having more educators to guide the process of learning.

The general lack of access to resources aside from the textbook presented a big concern for many students. Access to audio and additional practice exercises not only enhances learning but it maintains motivation. While a handful of students came to the first day of class with their own, generally very worn copies of Spanish–English dictionaries, I solicited donations for a few classroom copies. We used a traditional, pen-and-paper workbook that accompanied the text, with edits to make sure all activities were appropriate, but perhaps the biggest limitation was the lack of access to audio reinforcement, which is typically delivered through an Internet-based "workbook" with interactive tasks.

At this particular prison, we had something better: more than 400 native Spanish speakers. In the classroom, I frequently asked the teaching assistants to lead activities so that students could interact with native speakers of different regions and accents. "Más despacio por favor" (more slowly please) was a phrase that everyone quickly learned.

Students were asked to conduct survey activities with native Spanish-speaking peers outside of the classroom. One simple activity involved asking a peer his name, where he was from, and his age in Spanish with the help of a worksheet. This simple activity and others like it had an effect that no one anticipated. Lines of communication between primarily African-Americans and Latinos were opened as students sought help with homework or test preparation. Especially motivated students challenged themselves to regular conversations with their peers, and study partnerships began to form. Even the correctional officers began using the Spanish that they knew when interacting with students and native Spanish speakers. One student let me know that he and an officer discussed the contents of the day's menu in Spanish at length.

This connection between students and the Hispanic community of the prison at large was especially useful as we continued to offer additional Spanish courses. It made up for the lack of "extra practice" exercises and even replaced them with something more valuable: one-on-one interaction with native speakers. While no attempt was made to assess cultural learning, it can be argued that, especially among the more advanced Spanish students, cultural exchange took place through the sharing of experiences and histories.

One of the most meaningful contributions of one teaching assistant, Erick Nava Palomino, who himself had earned two associate's degrees through the community college and was now working on his bachelor's degree through the University of Illinois, was the delivery of a simple activity. The grammar focus of the activity was to use the verb *faltar* or, *to lack,* in Spanish. This verb necessitates the use of an indirect object pronoun, which is often challenging for students. For example, *Me falta dinero* means, literally, *I lack money* or *I don't have money.*

The activity was designed for college students and asked them to identify what they lacked when they came to college. Some of the options included study skills, money, good habits. Before beginning the activity, Erick explained that the class would be discussing what they lacked when they came to prison and elicited more options from students. Common sense, discipline, and family support were some of the responses given. At the end of the activity, many students had shared their experiences of coming to prison and what contributed to their journey—*in Spanish!* Students talked about lacking love and support from their family. They talked about their lack of self-awareness. And the fact that one of their peers was leading the activity encouraged even more engagement than if I were to have led the activity. It can be said that this ability to speak of one's experience had the potential of opening up further channels of communication with the monolingual Spanish speakers at the prison, an effect I had not even considered when I took on the class initially.

Reflections of the Instructor on the Program

By the time I left the position at Danville, I had offered six courses in three different levels of Spanish, including an informal "Spanish for Heritage Speakers" group, and reached more than 100 students. Many students began studying in these courses with very minimal knowledge of Spanish, though as they continued through the series of courses many left the program near fluency. The individuals who achieved such success were typically motivated to seek interaction with Spanish speakers outside of the classroom, look for opportunities to read more in Spanish, and even engage in self-study between courses. Students at the prison were familiar with community college courses that were technical, including automotive, wood shop, or custodial maintenance; one student on the last day of class shared with me how he felt this course was, for him, more like those technical courses. He stated that he really learned the language and would be using it in his future employment.

Of course not all students responded as positively. My philosophy of language teaching involves using the target language *exclusively* in class, which presents challenges of its own, in or out of the prison environment. Students needed to be sold on the methodology as well as convinced of its efficacy. Less outgoing students are often quite reluctant to participate, and frequent "pep talks" were required. In addition, I gave students frequent opportunities to give me feedback in the form of midterm evaluations. Without traditional office hours (which were not possible in the prison) this form of communication proved indispensable.

During my time as an instructor at Danville, I felt strongly about adapting materials to the experience of my students, so activities about dorm rooms became about cells, going out on the weekend became about sports activities available to my incarcerated students. From time to time, a less "realistic" activity would slip through and we would complete it.

One activity asked students to design their dream vacation. Where would they go? Who would they go with? What would they do there? Students became particularly excited about these activities and the freedom to imagine that it gave them.

At other times perhaps I would not have time to adapt an activity and we would simply use the book exercises that were designed for typical college students. At one point I apologized for not having adapted the activity and asking them to do it anyway. I will never forget the response of one student: "You don't always have to remind us where we are." This is a prison lesson to be remembered when constructing the type of pedagogy I have proposed here.

Were I to teach again in a correctional environment, supplemental activities would include both those that reflected current realities and future plans (apartment hunting, for example) as well as activities like the above-described vacation activity that allows students a temporary respite from their current incarcerated state. As I hope I've conveyed here, due to the constraints of teaching in a prison environment, it is essential that a language instructor make teaching and learning a community effort, and not place him or herself as the sole instructor, an "Atlas" holding the world on his or her shoulders. Native Spanish speakers have to play a role in the classroom to mitigate the large class size and lack of access to materials, including speaking and listening activities. Their inclusion in teaching and learning, as I've described, has the secondary, positive effect of enriching community and building relationships within the institution.

Reflections of a Teaching Assistant on the Program, by Erick Nava Palomino

In this section, I will introduce my perspective as one of the participants in the program. I was an incarcerated university student with a vision of becoming a teacher upon release, and I therefore saw the opportunity of being a teaching assistant in a community college class as an invaluable way of gaining authentic classroom experience while at the same time helping an instructor who had participated in the training I received through the University of Illinois to become an English-as-a-second-language instructor—a topic for another day. I recognized that as a native Spanish speaker, I would be valued for my knowledge and experience of the Spanish language. Also, being incarcerated, I knew how to make the classroom a more comfortable place for the students to acquire a second language, because I was one of them. The students asked me questions that they otherwise would not have asked the White female Spanish teacher. From the beginning of the program, we knew that we lacked most of the technological resources that "free" college students had, so we knew having Spanish-speaking teaching assistants would prove invaluable. As native Spanish speakers, we brought our knowledge, pronunciation, and culture of the language, which made the language acquisition process more authentic.

But all the training and experience that we received as teaching assistants became of less importance once I recognized what it meant to my family, to my peers, and to me that I could, as an incarcerated man, serve in a role as an educator. I don't know exactly when it happened but as the classes went on I began to feel a type of redemption, due to the fact that I was able to positively contribute to my community and that I was entrusted to do so regardless of my background. This to me was the biggest reward of being a teaching assistant in prison.

Within the classroom, we were more than peers to the students as we took the role of instructors and mentors. This was groundbreaking, because before these classes some men would not talk to each other, let alone ask each other for assistance, due to past neighborhood conflicts that continued while in prison. The intergroup animosity was forgotten in the Spanish classroom as we all tried to facilitate the learning and teaching of a second language. Through this process, I saw that my hope of becoming a teacher upon release was a true possibility. As we walked around the class to help individual students out and as we presented certain activities to the class, I saw that students looked to us for guidance and trusted us to help them to the best of our abilities. Seeing how the instructor trusted us to lead a class activity, grade tests and homework, and participate in oral exams was transformative, because it showed us that we were worthy of trust.

Outside the classroom, the mentoring and tutoring continued as students saw the teaching assistants in the yard, the dining hall, or the dayroom (common room) and transformed any location within the prison into a classroom. Even during visiting hours, students would introduce us to their families, use what they had learned in class, and say things like "that's my Spanish teacher" or "he's teaching me Spanish." Besides the extra tutoring that happened outside the classroom, what amazed me the most was the sense of community that was created as non-English-speaking Mexican men interacted with students from the Spanish class, who were mostly African-American and White, as they asked for help or tried to complete a homework assignment that required them to interview a native Spanish speaker. Because of the language barrier as well as the race and culture barrier, these groups of men tended not to interact or socialize with each other. But because of the Spanish class, these groups of men were able to communicate and eventually in some cases become friends. The teaching instructors acting as ambassadors helped create foundations of friendships between these groups of men who until now had limited interactions with each other.

They also recognized the effort the teaching assistants were making to try to help them learn a new language and therefore showed a level of respect that might otherwise not have been there. They started to see us teaching assistants as leaders whom they could ask for help about Spanish or for advice about daily life.

It was powerful to have incarcerated men participate as teaching assistants for others at the prison who, rather than gain trust or encouragement to better themselves, looked toward the future through the experience of oppression and dehumanization of prison. This prison culture had created a mistrust of any institutional personnel or program. Becoming a teaching assistant empowered you to show your peers, family, and the administration of the prison that we could do something positive and productive, regardless of our pasts. A side effect of being a teaching assistant was that our peers saw in us the potential that they all had in themselves to do something positive while in prison. They saw a potential that many had not seen until they saw their peers teaching a college class. They saw a future for themselves where they too could one day be a teaching assistant while in prison, instead of just a worker used for manual labor. These ideas led to ideas of them possibly being teachers once they got out, if they chose to do so. But more importantly, they saw that they too could be entrusted to help their communities and prepare themselves in the process to be productive citizens once released into society.

Being able to redeem yourself in the eyes of the community, which mistrusts you because of the lifestyle you chose to live before your incarceration, was a powerful motivation and reward to being a teaching assistant. The anticipation of returning to your nonmainstream community as a productive member of society also motivated each of us to work hard in the classroom. Not only the community would see us in a different light; our families began to see another side of us and to feel relief in the fact that we were doing something positive and in the idea that maybe we would actually do something productive once we were released. They began to see our personalities change as we took on the role of leadership within our peer group. Our families saw how students introduced us to their families as their teachers, and they saw how we were changing in a positive way. The happiness and relief in their eyes as we talked about the activities we led in the classroom and as we talked about our future plans once we would be released were priceless.

So yes, having Spanish-speaking teaching assistants in a Spanish class is vital because they are an invaluable resource who can be used to help the students as well as the teacher in the classroom. As a Spanish speaker, you bring the audio that free students would get from disks in their regular classroom. You bring the culture that free students typically get from having Internet access. You are the tutors whom free students could hire if they needed them. Teaching assistants also give the teachers a chance to rest within the four-hour classes. Having multiple teaching assistants also adds different teaching dynamics to the classroom, as each teaching assistant brings his or her own teaching style and personality to the classroom. Having a variety of teachers allows you to keep the classes interesting, because it breaks the monotony of having one teacher teach for four hours.

The act of giving incarcerated men the chance to become teaching assistants benefits both the community college instructors and the incarcerated students. This act of empowerment allows them to contribute to the world they live in by teaching students a new language, by being mentors and role models, and by becoming something that many never thought possible in the present prison complex, instead of just being unwilling victims who accept the things that are done to them. Through this act of empowerment, many began to believe that we were more than criminals not worthy of a second chance; we are intelligent and loving human beings who can still positively contribute to the world we exist in.

Concluding Remarks From Both Instructor and Teaching Assistant

While it is undoubtable that the prison classroom presents a number of challenges to learning and teaching, like those we have outlined here, it is crucial to recognize the human resource, incarcerated students, who are in a position to contribute their skills and knowledge to enrich the learning experience of their peers. To be able to offer such transformative experiences both to language students and to those who function as teaching assistants, the instructor must be willing to cede some control in the classroom and to not function as the sole decision maker, but to trust and to allow others to play an active role in the educational process.

Reference

VanPatten, B., Lee, J., Ballman, T. L., & Farley, A. (2007). ¿Sabías qué? New York, NY: McGraw-Hill Education.

ERICK NAVA PALOMINO *assisted in peer education at the Danville Correctional Center, and served as a teaching partner in the Language Partners program of the Education Justice Project, the college-in-prison program of the University of Illinois.*

LEE RAGSDALE *taught Spanish at the Danville Correctional Center for Danville Area Community College, and was a cofounder of the Language Partners program of the Education Justice Project, the college-in-prison program of the University of Illinois.*

5

In this chapter, an incarcerated student in Illinois discusses the issue of cheating/plagiarism in the prison context and weighs in on the value of vocational education compared to degree-granting academic programs in prison.

A Call for Cultural Democracy

Daniel E. Graves

The less you think about your oppression, the more your tolerance of it grows ... after a while, people just think oppression is the normal state of things. But to become free, you have to be acutely aware of being a slave.

(Shakur, 1987, p. 262)

The convict mentality, which includes the concepts of no snitching, them against us, and mind your own business, greatly inhibits the attainment of postsecondary education within prison. Another stumbling block for future educational and posteducational success of the convict is lowered standards and unwillingness of educators to think outside the traditional educational box. The age-old battle, Booker T. Washington versus W. E. B. DuBois, takes place in these vocational and academic classrooms, with Booker T. winning most rounds. The continued banking system of education, overused in high school, is being used here on a population of men with 25 being the median age. The tools that transform students into professionals are not given: no academic writing, no critical thinking, and no dialectic learning tools that most traditional college students either enter college with or obtain during their first few semesters, hence, the production of passing students whom the college is failing.

To Tell or Not to Tell

I am a rat, a stool pigeon, a snitch; I am one who has violated the "code" on at least one level, simply because I, after weeks of consideration, told. Ten years ago, seven years ago—or even five years ago—during my 21-plus years of incarceration, I never would have violated the code in any way.

NEW DIRECTIONS FOR COMMUNITY COLLEGES, no. 170, Summer 2015 © 2015 Wiley Periodicals, Inc.
Published online in Wiley Online Library (wileyonlinelibrary.com) • DOI: 10.1002/cc.20143

Now, because I know cheating only hurts the student, I step up and express my displeasure with cheating and cheaters.

The "code" allowed students to approach me freely out of earshot of the instructor and say things like: "If I wasn't able to cheat I never would have passed that test" or "I'm glad she doesn't know about the computer giving the right answers or we'd be out there." The students tell me these things fully aware that I am not a student but a teacher's aide in the college vocational program. The students feel they can tell me these things because my allegiance to them and my Department of Corrections (DOC) institutional number convey the fact that I have been in prison for a long time, and thus say that I am on their side and won't snitch. Because all teachers are staff, outsiders who do their eight and go home, they are not us—so they, though we're to trust they're educating us properly, are not to be trusted. The outsiders have the ability to hit the panic switch and have anyone of the cons—student or aide—kicked out of the course, sent to segregation, out of the institution, or simply punished unjustly. A power dynamic exists. Staff, no matter their uniform, have all the power, for roughly 90% of inmate disciplinary reports are lost by the offender. Even when wrong, staff sticks together in their persecution of convicts. The authority wielded over us makes it an us-versus-them situation at all times.

My six-character institutional number begins with a B, which tells everyone who understands the system that I entered the DOC between 1989 and 1996 (there are very few exceptions to this numbering rule). My number informs staff and inmates that I have either been locked up approximately 20 years or that I am a recidivist; either way, the code, learned in that time frame, was universally upheld, remembered, practiced, displayed. Because I am from that era, respect is due. My number also says that no matter what I see another con do, I am supposed to turn a blind eye (there are few exceptions to this rule).

The advent of mass incarceration has ushered in a culture—the prison culture—not understood by outsiders (staff). This culture puts a greater premium on the sheet of paper received after an accomplishment (i.e., a certificate) than on the daunting road taken, and the experience gained, while achieving said reward. Hence rises the idea of getting that certificate by any means. After all, the judge, parole board, and counselors wrongly look at the accomplishments, not the deeds that led thereto; plus, a certificate, no matter how it is gained, may, in some instances, mean the difference in serving an additional 90 days or 180 days. Ironically, the sentence reduction is called "good conduct credit." So it is understandable why inmates try to pass these courses as quickly and easily as possible, but does that make cheating acceptable even if I don't agree with the mode of a banked-in education?

Though there is no justification for the "cheating" as a road to getting out of jail sooner, there is a culture that has developed within this new prison environment that needs to be addressed. A cultural democracy[1] in which the act of critical pedagogy is enacted to address the true needs of these men is a must. The new ideological concept of "achieve so I can leave" has supplanted the essentiality of learning, and the instructors' lack of interest in engaging the students and not simply banking them only adds to this systemic malfunction.

Booker T. Is Kicking W.E.B.'s Butt

Too much stress is placed on vocational education in prison. Learning a specific trade in one specific field is limiting, especially for a newly released prisoner who needs any job as opposed to waiting on a job in the area of his banked-in vocation. These college courses are watered down at best, too easy at least, with my greatest hope being that college courses on the outside mirror nothing of the junior college experience of the inside.

Dan Colson taught the first bachelor-level course I had taken. Even though I had six vocational certificates and associate's degrees in art, science, and general education, Professor Colson taught me that I didn't really know a thing about academic success. I soon learned that I was ill-prepared for a true undergraduate-level classroom. Nothing taught *to* me in any course prior to Professor Colson's had prepared me to think critically. In a dialectic learning classroom, where the expression of all voices and ideas was encouraged, I learned that my personal thoughts and emotions, which are aroused while engaging with particular texts, were important. Professor Colson shut me down as I began regurgitating (summarizing) text read for class. "Yeah, yeah, yeah I know what the book says, I read it. I want to know what you think about it." I was good at receiving what was deposited in my head and recalling it for joke-able "college level" multiple choice, matching, short answer, and true/false tests. However, being asked how I felt, what I thought, was mind blowing. I was ill prepared for Professor Colson, who, it seemed to me, was an abnormal educator. Because I didn't know how to perform in such a space, yet still wanted to participate, I forced myself to stammer through thoughts. I wrote notes (never before then) to take to class to challenge myself, the class, and the professor. For the same course, we all had to write a seven- to ten-page essay. Not a problem, I thought. I'm still revising that paper more than five years later. Though it was handed in, graded, and returned, I still pick up that paper weekly and see so many errors it's laughable—one of those laughs used to fight back tears. Poor grammar, bad sentence structure, misplaced punctuation, just about all possible writing violations are present therein. Yet I handed in my initial draft knowing (thinking) it was perfect, because I had gotten away with the exact same effort in previous college courses. Three revisions later, and because the course was ending, I still turned in subpar work. Why? Because none of my instructors up until then ever told me I was wrong, nor did I ever fail due to inadequate work. Because I had been poorly educated, and continually educated poorly, where one bad student goes from one bad educator to another and not one of the educators takes the initiative to fix a deeply broken student, or a broken system.

Conclusion

I am critical of the vocational and poorly delivered academic mode of educational programming, because I am a product thereof. As a product of that system, one that is failing men by not allowing or nurturing critical intellectual growth, I now see the gaffes I was allowed to take, the missteps instructors, with different faces yet similar modalities, are allowing this new wave of prison students to take. To provide sustenance to an eager mind, a mind that thirsts for a challenge, is transformative. In prison, where the monotony of daily life and the escape therefrom are instances of inevitability and never-ending circular dilemmas, education should be a freedom, not a greater form of incarceration.

In a teaching space where bodies are trapped, captive, lacking the ability and the freedom to move mentally, physically, or spiritually, educators should aim at liberating the trapped, incarcerated, indoctrinated minds. Intellectually, I make up the whole of all the bits and pieces picked up in my life. The concept of education as this bolt here, this nut there, fails the naturally active mind miserably. Vocational education, to prisoners, is a barbed pill. I do understand how trades can possibly help ex-cons be successful on the outside. Vocational training does serve a purpose, and the numbers of vocational certificates handed out to prisoners speaks to both the thirst for higher education in prison and the get-out-of-jail-by-any-means-necessary mantra of the new generation of inmates. I would trade in more than 200 credit hours of vocational training for a bachelor's degree.

We lack critical pedagogy. There is a deficiency of critical thinking, critical thought. The current crops of "higher education" in prison junior college courses, from my experience, are wanting. These programs are wanting in the way of not supplying that true sustenance for success—critical success, thinking-outside-of-the-box success. Students are being taught into a box, and isn't a box similar to a cage?

Note

1. "The term cultural democracy reflects the perspective and philosophy of Ramirez and Castaneda (1974). Cultural democracy pertains to an educational philosophy that affirms the right of individuals to be educated in their own language and learning style and the right to maintain a bicultural identity—that is, to retain an identification with their culture of origin while integrating, in a constructive manner, the institutional values of the dominant culture" (Darder, 1995, p. xvi).

References

Darder, A. (1995). *Culture and power in the classroom: A critical foundation for bicultural education*. New York, NY: Bergin and Garvey.
Shakur, A. (1987). *Assata: An autobiography*. Chicago, IL: Lawrence Hill.

DANIEL E. GRAVES was a member of the inaugural cohort of students enrolled in undergraduate classes through the Education Justice Project, the college-in-prison program of the University of Illinois.

NEW DIRECTIONS FOR COMMUNITY COLLEGES • DOI: 10.1002/cc

6

This chapter describes the author's experience teaching ethnic studies inside a unique California prison, and calls for college-in-prison educators to engage culturally appropriate curricula to realize the full transformative potential of the prison classroom.

The Transformative Power of Sankofa: Teaching African History Inside San Quentin State Prison

Nathaniel B. D. Moore

This course should be relevant in everyone's life because it is a piece of history that shaped the world. There's an old saying "you don't know where you're going until you know where you come from." This is where I was in life until I took this course. The understanding I received of myself and the self-worth of knowing that I came from a rich tradition gave me a lot of self-worth and pride.[1]

Sankofa is a cultural concept from the Akan people of Ghana and Cote d'Ivoire. Translated from Twi, it literally means "go back and get it," or "return and get it." Figuratively, it symbolizes the importance of knowing one's past to build a successful future. Similar ideas can be found in societies around the world, and it is these cultural principles that buttress the empowering educational content of ethnic studies. Developed from the shared historical experiences of exploitation, racism, and colonialism between Black, Latino/a, Native American, and Asian American students in the 1960s, ethnic studies courses create space for students to define and shape their own identities, self-worth, and sense of community—and can strengthen communities that have been and continue to be devastated by mass incarceration. By examining the positive effects teaching ethnic histories has on identity development and community building, this chapter explores the transformative potential of culturally relevant education and reorients Sankofa from an abstract idea into a sustainable component of required prison-in-college curricula. I will discuss my experiences

NEW DIRECTIONS FOR COMMUNITY COLLEGES, no. 170, Summer 2015 © 2015 Wiley Periodicals, Inc.
Published online in Wiley Online Library (wileyonlinelibrary.com) • DOI: 10.1002/cc.20144

teaching an African history course inside California's San Quentin State Prison; analyze student reactions to the material; review the positive effects of the course as related to identity development and community building; and finally suggest some best practices moving forward.

The Setting

San Quentin State Prison is located in affluent Marin County, California, a short drive from both Oakland and San Francisco. Most of California's state prisons offer very few opportunities for personal development. Alcoholics Anonymous, Narcotics Anonymous, a GED program, and perhaps some minimal vocational training are all most of California's approximately 135,000 prisoners can expect, if that much (California Department of Corrections and Rehabilitation, 2014). However, San Quentin is "unique" in that about half of its 4,000 prisoners are eligible to participate in programming, often involving outside volunteers who sponsor, facilitate, and work collaboratively with more than 50 groups. This includes the only on-site, degree-granting higher education program in all of California's 33 state prisons. The nonprofit Prison University Project (PUP) runs the college program at San Quentin, an extension site of Patten University, a small for-profit university in Oakland, California. PUP offers a tuition-free accredited associate of arts degree and serves hundreds of students per semester. As of June 2013, more than 100 men have graduated with associate's degrees (Prison University Project, n.d.).

Before engaging the course itself, it is imperative to discuss the insidious system of racial segregation that is simply part of daily life inside of California's prisons. This system is composed of a myriad of legal and unofficial rules, often varying by institution. Utilized by prison staff, de jure policies include race-based lockdowns, the prohibition of mixed-race cells, and the official racial classification of all prisoners. But de facto examples of racism, imposed by the prisoners on each other and supported by staff, include unofficial regulations on where one can work out or sit in the cafeteria, and with whom one can socialize. There can be severe sanctions for breaking the rules, including physical violence and/or death. The system of racial segregation is intended to breed distrust and emphasize difference among prisoners, disrupting solidarity and unity.

The Course

The most recent incarnation of the African history course was taught at San Quentin from January to May in both 2012 and 2013. I began volunteering with PUP in August 2013, and after a number of months, I noticed a lack of volunteers, classes, and academic content that represented African or African-American perspectives. When informed of the opportunity to coordinate and teach a history class of my choosing, I excitedly offered to teach

NEW DIRECTIONS FOR COMMUNITY COLLEGES • DOI: 10.1002/cc

African history. I was joined in this effort by a co-instructor, who played an important role in conceptualizing and supporting the course, without whom neither the class nor this paper would be possible. Collectively, we created a syllabus modeled on an introduction to African history course I previously taught at a four-year university in the Midwest, supplementing with resources and content we thought appropriate. In hindsight, the historical scope of the course was far too large, ranging from ancient African empires to the present. We covered a wide range of topics, including, but not limited to: precolonial African communities; African ways of knowing; traditional African political structures and religions; the transatlantic slave trade; African responses to colonialism; nationalist and independence movements; Pan-Africanism; structural adjustment; gender; civil society; and globalization.

These topics were engaged through assigned readings (mostly printed academic articles or photocopied book chapters), lectures, and full-class discussions. Students were also assigned novels—*A Man of the People* (Chinua Achebe) and *So Long a Letter* (Maimouna Ba)—and we watched the film *Amandla!* as a supplement to their weekly readings. Generally, the course was taught chronologically; the assigned readings presented historical background and/or focused on a specific event, culture, or country to illustrate a larger theme. The goal was for the lectures to fill in the blanks, connect the readings to important concepts, and facilitate discussion. Most of the assigned readings were drawn from scholarly articles whose authors generated little interest among the men, although we did assign chapters by more notable figures like Walter Rodney, Franz Fanon, and Steve Biko, which drew considerably more attention. In terms of graded work, students were required to write a midterm, a final, and essays about the assigned novels.

During those two semesters, classes of approximately 25–30 students met twice a week for a little less than two hours at a time. A majority of students identified as African-American and were between 30 and 50 years old, but we had a diversity of races and ages in both semesters. During both semesters, it took students a while to warm up and feel out the course, the instructors, and their fellow students. This was especially true in this class because of the potentially explosive racial dynamics surrounding discussions of issues like slavery and colonialism. This is not to give the impression that everyone was exactly on the same page at all times proclaiming the glory of African history, but by about halfway through the semester, we had collectively crafted a safe space where one could engage challenging issues without being worried about saying the wrong thing.

The actual classroom was a stand-alone trailer, within the education "campus," but separate from the education building. Two correctional officers were assigned to the education campus; however, because they sat in the education building, with the exception of a correctional officer entering class once a day for a head-count, we experienced no immediate supervision in the classroom. Our classroom was not particularly memorable. Random posters featuring motivational messages, health information, and *National Geographic* pullouts dotted the walls, and tables with two or three chairs each filled the room. There were two sets of windows allowing natural light to stream in and a large whiteboard on one wall that served as the focal point for instruction. There was also a computer that was off limits to volunteer instructors and students and sat idly near one set of windows.

Before discussing the positive effects of the class on identity development and community building, I want to focus on a couple aspects of critical student feedback. Two of the main critiques of the course were that it tried to cover way too much and was sometimes too academic. Because we covered so much history so quickly, we rarely got a chance to really take an in-depth look at anything and often had to simplify complex processes, ideas, and events. This tended to frustrate students, especially if they found something of particular interest or did not understand it fully. Furthermore, especially the first year, many articles were far too detailed, dense, and narrowly focused. Finding comprehensive yet easy-to-read readings remained a challenge throughout, and students seemed to get more from shorter selections from more notable figures, novels, the film, and class lectures and discussions.

Identity Development.

> I did not know anything about my African roots and now I know the basics that I can carry with me for the rest of my life. They were educators, innovators, and growing in technological advancements before the Cross-Atlantic slave trade and the European colonization of Africa.

One of the foremost positive effects of an African history course, and all culturally relevant courses, is identity development. The majority of each class's students were African-American, and one reason so many signed up was that they were interested in engaging their heritage. Although some students had a detailed knowledge about various aspects of African history, many through self-study, the majority knew of Africa mostly through the media and/or K–12 schooling. The media they had been exposed to at best lacked depth and complexity, and at worst portrayed Africans living in jungles with apes or other destructive stereotypes. Most students reported that they never learned about Africa in school, and if they did, it focused solely on the slave trade. Each semester, the classroom became an empowering space for students of African descent to (re)discover and engage with their identity.

> I will probably forget most of the Algebra I learned here in Patten and have already forgotten most of the statistics and philosophy I studied. But I still remember a lot about African history because it was presented as the story

of people and their endurance under harsh and oppressive conditions. As a prisoner for over thirty years, I feel that the history of Africans is a part of my history.

In addition to discovering new dimensions to a continent's history, students were able to articulate interesting linkages between class content and their own ideas of self, drawing conceptual and at times literal connections between class topics and their own lives. For example, our in-class viewing and discussion of the film *Amandla!* allowed students to relate their own experiences of incarceration with the experience of those incarcerated in South Africa's prisons. The documentary, through a chronological history of the South African liberation struggle, shows the role music played in the fight against apartheid. Songs and music served to unite those fighting for freedom, console those who were incarcerated, and create an effective underground form of communication. A sizable portion of the documentary focuses on the use of music to strengthen the resolve of those then locked inside South Africa's prisons. In addition to engaging the history of South Africa in a manner that spoke to their lived experiences, students were able to connect with the content in a much deeper and more relevant way than simply memorizing facts, dates, and names. Cultural histories allow for educational experiences like these and facilitate larger developments in identity and how students see and understand themselves.

As I learned African history, I was able to appreciate the history of my land, of my people's from a whole new perspective. I was provided with information that helped me understand, why my country, my people, is what it is today. I understood better why my country is a third world country, and why third world countries exist in the first place.

A cornerstone of ethnic studies, among the most exhilarating aspects of identity development in the course was seeing and hearing about cross-cultural connections stimulated by the content. Students of Latino/a, Asian, and Native heritage often traced themes and events in African history to their own histories, linking their identities with those of the African diaspora. One of the most interesting classes involving the commonalities of colonial legacies centered on comparing and contrasting the colonial occupations of Vietnam by the French and of Ghana by the British. The students of Asian descent were extremely engaged, and the conversations between them and the students of African ancestry were rich with a legacy of shared struggle. African history, as well as Latino/a, Native American, and Asian history, is beneficial not just for the students who ethnically identify with the content but also for all those who want to transcend racial classifications and build more human connections.

NEW DIRECTIONS FOR COMMUNITY COLLEGES • DOI: 10.1002/cc

Community Building.

> In our community here, we can talk about issues in Africa with the under-
> standing we have from this class. Had we not taken this class, it would have
> been very unlikely anyone of us would use African history as an example in
> informal discussions on the yard. Africa is part of our worldview now, and a
> subject discussed between the Asian and Pacific Islanders here.

Another important component of ethnic studies is building understanding of the ways colonialism has impacted communities of color, both
domestically and internationally, and the ways rich ethnic histories have
been marginalized and subjugated by those in power. The African history
course and the material that accompanied it facilitated community building
both inside and outside the classroom. Students formed study groups with
their classmates that grew to accommodate even those who were not taking the course but were interested in the material. The prison newspaper,
The San Quentin News, ran stories on Africa throughout the duration of the
course, and students in the class taped an interview with me and my co-
instructor that was rebroadcast on the San Quentin's internal TV station.
The modest media attention galvanized further excitement about African
history, as well as general interest in the college program. Many men I had
never met approached me, interested in signing up for the college program
because they wanted to take African history, or stopped me on the yard to
share information, engage in conversation, or ask a question about the continent. All of these responses are indicative of a community built around a
common engagement with Africa.

> Yes I have shared this information! I felt it was of the upmost importance
> to enlighten my Goddaughter as to her history and to her self-worth as a
> descendent of African women. My Goddaughter attends the same schools
> that I myself attended; knowing this, I felt that it was necessary to give her
> [a young woman of 14–15] more of a reason to follow all her dreams no
> matter what obstacles stand in her way. Her response was to say thank you,
> and to let me know she was glad to read something more about Africa.

Many students indicated that they shared the information they learned
with their families. In addition to further substantiating the importance of
the course, this demonstrated larger impacts felt outside the prison walls,
such as strengthening family ties and, in some cases, correcting misinformation about one's heritage. One of the most impressive linkages between class
content and family occurred when we read selections from Walter Rodney's
How Europe Underdeveloped Africa. Students learned that the slave trade did
not just affect those taken captive; it also had massive effects on those who
remained behind in Africa. The social violence that accompanied the slave
trade created an environment of constant fear, discouraged technological

and intellectual innovation, and devastated communal bonds. Many students connected what happened to the social fabric of African communities to what their communities and families were experiencing. Students highlighted the destruction of family structure; the restriction of cultural, artistic, and intellectual production; and shifting economic and gender roles as indicators that the same social processes plaguing their communities had once plagued Africa. Again, these connections not only reinforce the relevancy of this content to our students' lives, but also allow students to contribute to their families' well-being and intellectual development despite being incarcerated.

The most exciting part of offering ethnic histories inside prison classrooms is its enormous transformative potential. Ethnic studies courses provide an empowering space for students to engage in personal development as well as larger community building. Ethnic studies classes not only provide a safe space to generate dialogue and dispel misinformation, but also provide a platform for transracial solidarity around parallel struggles. This space is essential in challenging the divisive racial conditions inside U.S. prisons. Daily life inside prison is intended to dehumanize and isolate, and it is vital that we cultivate spaces that allow students to make connections with one another, dismantle stereotypes about fellow students and the larger world, cultivate critical thinking, and celebrate commonalities.

Challenges and Best Practices

This section describes the challenges and best practices of the course.

Using Liberation Pedagogy in Prison.   Certainly one of the most challenging elements of college-in-prison is implementing innovative and revolutionary pedagogies. A primary influence on my teaching philosophy is Paulo Freire (1970). Unfortunately, prison classrooms leave much to be desired in terms of implementing his pedagogy. For example, despite cultivating a safe space to challenge racism, students still maintained the unofficial segregation policies by sitting with men of the same race in class, speaking to the fact that while classrooms can be pivotal spaces for empowerment, classrooms in and of themselves do not change prison policies or politics. Additionally, attempts to disrupt the student–instructor power dynamic proved complex. Students made it clear that group work was not wanted, and students all sat at tables facing me and I stood in front of the class, clearly replicating a regrettable instructor–student/free–incarcerated power dynamic. In addition, because I was the instructor, possessed an advanced degree and had visited southern Africa, I became the authority on all things African. This occurred even though I was the youngest person in the room and, while I am African-American, was born and have lived my entire life in the United States. In addition, institutional restrictions surrounding student behavior, instructor–student relationships, and content are considerable barriers. However, while a full-scale implementation of Paulo Freire's

NEW DIRECTIONS FOR COMMUNITY COLLEGES • DOI: 10.1002/cc

teaching practices may not be possible, it is imperative that we utilize the small spaces we can create to their fullest potential. Critical thinking, with the ultimate goal of social transformation, should be the foremost goal of every course taught inside prison, and program administrators and instructors should be committed to making sure their curricula are driven by sensitivity and relevancy to their students' current situations.

Commitment and Creativity. Truly integrating ethnic histories into college-in-prison courses will take a major commitment from directors, staff, and instructors. Some of the foremost challenges facing prison-in-college programs are a lack of space, lack of regular paid instructors, and an obligation to align with classic community college curriculum. These challenges do not mean that ethnic histories cannot find a place in college programs; it just means that we have to be more creative as to how to fit these classes in the curriculum. For example, most if not all degree-granting college-in-prison programs have some history requirement. There is no reason that ethnic histories can't fulfill U.S. or global history requirements. Humanities offerings can support relevant content: English courses on ethnic authors, communication courses built around relevant issues, sociology courses focusing on colonialism, and the like. In the same ways we embrace creativity to run science labs and produce poetry compilations, we need to learn to embrace creativity as it relates to culturally relevant courses.

Sustainability.   January 2012 was not the first time African history was offered by PUP. During the first semester, I learned from the men inside that another African history class had been offered many years ago. Upon exploration, I was able to contact the former instructor and, in speaking with her, learned that the course had last been offered in 1997, that her focus was the history of South Africa, and that there were many similarities in our learning objectives.

While it was good to learn that African history had been offered in the past, it was disappointing to learn there had been little effort to sustain or reoffer the course between 1997 and 2012. The only reason the course was offered in 2012 was that I suggested it and volunteered to teach it. Had I not, it would not have been offered. While this speaks to the previous comments on genuine commitment, it also speaks to the need for college-in-prison programs to conduct outreach and sustain culturally relevant instructors, resources, and courses. As indicated earlier, in a prison context ethnic histories are potentially more transformative than other academic courses, so programs should dedicate at least equal resources to sustaining these courses as they would to mathematics, psychology, or English.

Conclusion

Mass incarceration has done tremendous damage to Black, Brown, and poor communities across the United States and—however well intentioned— college-in-prison will not alleviate the stranglehold that mass incarceration

New Directions for Community Colleges • DOI: 10.1002/cc

has on these communities. However, offering ethnic histories that seek to link the common struggles of those incarcerated, discredit the divisive racial rhetoric of prison, and empower students to develop their own identities and communities, can be enormously beneficial for our students. In addition to positive identity development and community building, ethnic histories serve as a foundation for students to better understand and respond to the historical and contemporary processes that influence their lives and devastate their communities. In efforts to contribute to building a better future for all members of our society, we as educators must be willing to engage the concept of Sankofa and its cultural importance when designing college-in-prison curricula, choosing course offerings, and conducting outreach. Doing so will undoubtedly improve the impact and relevancy of community college programs in prison and deepen our resolve to create content that addresses the perspectives, histories, and lived experiences of our students.

Note

1. All quotes that appear in this chapter were taken from an anonymous questionnaire sent to all former students in October 2013. The questionnaire elicited open-end responses to the following five questions: (1) Regardless of your ethnicity, do you see yourself or the history of your people differently since taking the course? How so? (2) Have you shared any of the information you learned from the course with others? How did these people respond? (3) Do you view race or ethnicity differently since taking the course? How so? (4) What, if any, impact did this course have on your everyday life? and (5) Do you believe that this is course relevant to your life? If so, why?

References

California Department of Corrections and Rehabilitation. (2014). *Monthly report of population*. Retrieved from http://www.cdcr.ca.gov/Reports_Research/Offender_Information_Services_Branch/Monthly/TPOP1A/TPOP1Ad1404.pdf
Freire, P. (1970). *Pedagogy of the oppressed*. New York, NY: Continuum Press.
Prison University Project. (n.d.). *Academics*. Retrieved from http://www.prisonuniversityproject.org/academics

NATHANIEL B. D. MOORE is an archivist at the Freedom Archives in San Francisco; he served as an instructor and program assistant to the Prison University Project at San Quentin State Prison.

7

This chapter calls for educators to specifically engage the needs of African-American men, who often comprise the largest demographic in prison, in what the author calls the Humiliation-to-Humility Perspective.

Developing a Prison Education Pedagogy

Tony Gaskew

I must admit, when Attorney General Eric Holder recently announced the results of the study *Evaluating the Effectiveness of Correctional Education: A Meta-Analysis of Programs That Provide Education to Incarcerated Adults* (Davis, Bozick, Steele, Saunders, & Miles, 2013), as a prison educator I was both somewhat embarrassed and energized. Embarrassed that empirical data had to be produced before the "masses" could accept the reality that prison-based educational programming impacts the tangible and intangible life choices made by incarcerated students. As a tenured faculty member at the University of Pittsburgh-Bradford (UPB) and volunteer college educator at Federal Bureau of Prisons (BOP) FCI McKean over the past six years, this correlation was a no-brainer. Energized that now we can collectively begin to focus on the real challenges facing postsecondary prison programming—the who, what, where, when, why, and how of social justice accountability—in this chapter, I will briefly examine two of these challenges: (1) Who, from an institutional standpoint today, is best suited to provide postsecondary educational opportunities for our incarcerated Black students? and (2) How, from a pedagogical perspective, will our incarcerated Black students be educated?

Who Will Be the Gatekeepers of Postsecondary Prison Programming

Overall, as we stand today institutionally in higher education, community colleges are better suited to meet the educational needs of incarcerated students. Just to clarify, I do not mean to suggest that traditional four-year universities are not active participants in prison education programming because this would be the furthest thing from the truth; however,

NEW DIRECTIONS FOR COMMUNITY COLLEGES, no. 170, Summer 2015 © 2015 Wiley Periodicals, Inc.
Published online in Wiley Online Library (wileyonlinelibrary.com) • DOI: 10.1002/cc.20145

community colleges currently have the "cultural" advantages on three critical points.

First, community colleges have proximity to correctional facilities. There are roughly 1,200 community colleges spread across the nation, and I would challenge anyone to locate a correctional facility that is not within a reasonable driving distance from a community college (American Association of Community Colleges, 2014). Community college campuses can be found from the most isolated rural locations to the largest metropolitan cities across America, and everywhere in between. The closer the college campus to the correctional facility, the easier it will be to build, maintain, and develop long-term positive and mutually beneficial trusting relationships. There is no greater factor in the success of a postsecondary prison education program than trust, and this takes time, patience, and flexibility from all stakeholders.

Second, community colleges lower the cost of providing an education. In June 2014, I submitted a grant proposal to initiate the University of Pittsburgh at Bradford Prison Education Program (UPBPEP). My goal was to obtain grant funding that would provide 10 incarcerated students currently serving their prison sentences at FCI McKean an opportunity to complete a specialized program that could lead to an associate of arts degree from the University of Pittsburgh. The total cost of my grant request exceeded a quarter of a million dollars. However, funding for the same type of two-year postsecondary educational opportunity being offered by the Community College of Allegheny in Pennsylvania would only cost a fraction of that figure. Nationwide, the average tuition cost of completing 60 credit hours at a community college is $4,733, compared to $17,780 for an in-state public university (American Association of Community Colleges, 2014). The tuition cost for the same credit hours at a private university can exceed $60,000. Just to be clear, the opportunity to obtain a degree from the University of Pittsburgh or any top-tier research university is not and should not be cheap; however, the sustainability of prison-based education funding presents additional challenges.

Finally, and the most critical *cultural advantage*, community colleges traditionally serve an audience that is more diverse. Currently, community colleges nationwide educate the majority of "Black and Brown students." According to the National Center for Education Statistics (2014), Black and Hispanic Americans represented 16.2% and 19.4% of community college students, respectively. In fact, more than 36% of their students are first-generation college attendees. As well, almost 20% of their faculty consisted of "people of color."

Given that almost 80% of the 2.2 million offenders currently housed inside our nation's jails and prisons have never seen the inside of a college classroom in their lives, and that you're looking to educate an incarcerated audience that consists of nearly a 40% Black male population, pedagogically speaking, race does matter.

NEW DIRECTIONS FOR COMMUNITY COLLEGES • DOI: 10.1002/cc

This brings us to our second and most critical challenge: how, from a pedagogical perspective will our incarcerated Black students be educated?

The Pedagogical Racial Gap

Similar to traditional educational settings, one of the most glaring questions that continue to remain unanswered in classrooms behind prison walls is the pedagogical approach that best serves the needs and interests of the incarcerated student. Today, due to an unprecedented 700% rise in our nation's prison population over the past four decades, largely fueled by dysfunctional and biased drug enforcement strategies, our prison college classrooms are filled with young Black males. Nearly 40% of the "faces and voices" currently housed in our nations jails and prisons "live" the Black American experience, which includes more than 830,000 Black males (West, Sabol, & Greenman, 2011). Since the start of the correctional "Golden Age" in the early 1970s, the critical pedagogical movement has been infused into the foundation of postsecondary prison programming (Ryan & McCabe, 1994). The most distinguishing claim of the *Freirean* approach is that it is both "a form of cooperative educational practice and a form of collective educational action" for its practitioners (Forbes & Kaufman, 2008, p. 27). Critical pedogogists suggest that they not only encourage a learning environment that recognizes micro- and macrolevel power imbalances that create oppressive social structures both on the inside and outside of the classroom, but that they are also moved to change these power imbalances.

However, an ever-growing body of literature has raised some serious questions and supports a tempered skepticism into the "critical pedagogical movement," largely due to the field's dismissive analytical inclusion and application toward race and racism (Bell, 1992; Foster, 1997; Irvine, 1988, 1990; Leonardo, 2005; Lynn, 1999; Rossatto, Allen, & Pruyn, 2006). In the mid-1970s, motivated in large part by the inequalities of racism ingrained into our nation's legal system as applied to Black Americans, Derrick Bell developed what is known today as Critical Race Theory (CRT). Bell suggested that "we use a number of different voices, but all recognize that racial subordination maintains and perpetuates the American social order" (Delgado & Stefancic, 2005, p. 83). Critical race theory scholars argue that:

> CRT, as an analytical framework for addressing issues of social inequity, can be utilized as a way in which to uncover the racism embedded within American social structures and practices. More importantly, critical race theorists seek to reveal the hidden curriculum of racial domination and talk about the ways in which it is central to the maintenance of white supremacy. (Lynn, 2005, p. 129)

Bonilla-Silva (2005) suggests that the critical pedagogical framework is filled with foundational limitations regarding the conception of race and racism because its followers accept that: (a) Racism is excluded from the foundation or structure of the social system; (b) Racism is ultimately viewed as a psychological phenomenon to be examined at the individual level; (c) Racism is treated as a static phenomenon; (d) Racism is labeled as irrational and rigid; (e) Racism is understood as overt behavior; (f) Racism today is viewed as an remnant of the past historical racial situations; and (g) Racism is analyzed in a circular manner (pp. 3–6). *Reinventing Critical Pedagogy: Widening the Circle of Anti-Oppression Education* takes a critical tone at the dearth of Black scholars as inclusive participants in conferences, meetings, and classes, and as published authors and primary leaders within the critical pedagogical field. Allen (2006) goes on to suggest that most in the critical pedagogy community, who are primarily White, seem perfectly content with an academic audience that mirrors their own "faces and voices," adding:

> This troubles me deeply. How can the critical pedagogy community claim to be on the side of the oppressed when the members of the two most historically oppressed groups in the United States (and throughout the Americas), Blacks and Indians, don't show up to our events or have a strong, leading presence in critical pedagogy scholarship ... I would say that critical pedagogists, consciously or not, have been somewhat dismissive of all of those groups that ... are defined as the "collective Black" or those who are treated if they were Black ... [thus] if you ask those who consider themselves to be critical pedagogists to name the leaders in the field, the chances are great that most of the names will belong to Whites ... the point is Blacks aren't the primary leaders in the field; thus they aren't the major source of intellectual and political inspiration. But this situation shouldn't surprise us. I can't recall anyone in the community seriously asking, "Why aren't more Blacks ... or dark skinned people of color leading the field of critical pedagogy?" (pp. 4–6)

Thus, in an attempt to include the diverse voices of "Afrocentricity" (Asante, 2003) inside classrooms, numerous Black social justice scholars (Foster, 1997; Irvine, 1988, 1990; Lynn, 1999) guided the development of critical race pedagogy. Lynn (2005) noted that for Black educators, the emphasis of a critical race pedagogical movement involves:

> (1) Teaching children about the importance of African culture; (2) Dialogical engagement in the classroom; (3) Engaging in daily acts of self-affirmation; and (4) Resisting the challenging hegemonic administrators. (p. 128)

However, although critical race theory and critical race pedagogy provide solid frameworks to address the critical pedagogical "race problem" in traditional educational settings, there continues to be a dearth of approaches specifically designed to reach the Black incarcerated student. The *Humiliation to Humility Perspective* (HHP) was developed to fill this pedagogical gap. HHP is a flexible, connective, and "color conscious" approach that interjects the "lived" Black American experiences of incarcerated offenders into the ownership of knowledge, allowing Black males access to the truths behind their own cultural history, the criminal justice system, and victimization, inspiring true ownership to make life choices.

The Humiliation to Humility Perspective (HHP)

The HHP expands the pedagogical discussion of the "invisible three dimensional elephant inside the prison classroom": racism, White supremacy, and White privilege, by incorporating the narrative truths of the *lived* experiences of incarcerated Black males. hooks (2003, p. 93) emphasizes the need for educators to address the truths behind 400 years of the "politics of shaming, self-segregation, and transgenerational learned helplessness" within the Black American experience, which for one third of all adult Black males now includes membership as a living and breathing part of the "new Jim Crow" (Alexander, 2010). In *Teaching Community: A Pedagogy of Hope*, hooks (2003) adds:

> When educators evaluate why some students fail while others succeed they rarely talk about the role of shame as a barrier of learning … embedded in this notion of freedom is the assumption that access is all that is needed to create the conditions for equality. The thinking was to let black children go to the same schools as white peers and they will have all that is needed to be equal and free. Such thinking denies the role that devaluation and degradation, or all strategies of shaming, play in maintaining racial subordination, especially in the arena of education … African Americans have suffered and continue to suffer trauma, much of it the re-enactment of shaming. The self-segregation black folks do in integrated settings, particularly those where white people are the majority group, is a defense mechanism protecting them from being the victims of shaming assaults. (pp. 93–94)

Thus, for incarcerated Black men the pedagogical approach must reframe the transgenerational impact of racism, White supremacy, and White privilege into the *politics of shaming, self-segregation, and learned helplessness* that now includes the *lived journey of incarceration* that involves: (a) a disconnect in owning one's truth; (b) the separation and loss of one's cultural legacy; (c) the creation of *a Black counterculture of crime*; (d) the welcoming entrance into the criminal justice system; (e) the continued cycle of the victimization of Black children; and (f) the inability to make any transformative life choices. The HHP infuses these truths into a pedagogical framework that consists of five tenets that guide the approach: owning the truth; understanding your history; processing the criminal justice system; knowing the victims; and making tough choices (see Figure 7.1).

NEW DIRECTIONS FOR COMMUNITY COLLEGES • DOI: 10.1002/cc

Figure 7.1. Humiliation to Humility Perspective (HHP) Model

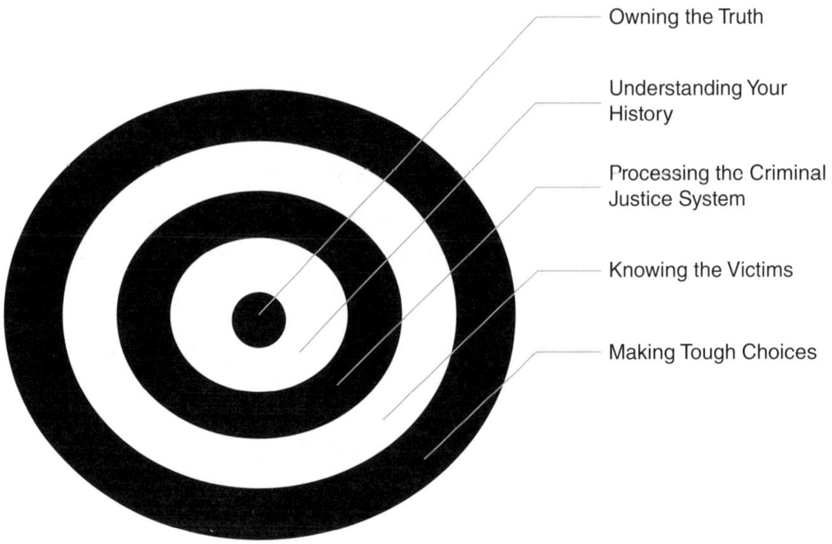

Owning the Truth

Understanding Your History

Processing the Criminal Justice System

Knowing the Victims

Making Tough Choices

Source: Image, design, and concept created by Tony Gaskew

Although I will discuss the basic framework of the HHP in this chapter, a complete and in-depth description can be found in my book, *Rethinking Prison Reentry: Transforming Humiliation into Humility* (Gaskew, 2014). As well, my emphasis using HHP in this chapter will only focus on incarcerated Black men. This is by no means a slight on the ugly truths facing Black women, who have also found themselves trapped in the same cycle of shame, self-segregation, and learned helplessness in mass incarceration. The unique "voices and narratives" of incarcerated Black women requires their own platform, which for reasons of brevity cannot be explored in this chapter.

First, the center of the HHP pedagogical approach rests with owning the truth. Incarcerated Black males have been systemically "lied to" their entire lives, so much, in fact, that many do not have any idea what the truth looks like, sounds like, tastes like, smells like, or feels like. However, for an incarcerated Black man to own his truth, he must first be encouraged to look into the polished metal mirror of his prison cell and ask himself, "How did I get here?" The concepts of W. E. B. Du Bois, Carter G. Woodson, Franklin E. Frazier, Marcus Garvey, John Henrik Clarke, Malcolm X, and other Black social justice scholars can help in this quest for truth. However, they can only be encouraged to seek this intellectual and moral truth in an educational setting where educators are prepared to share their own "lived" understanding of racism, White supremacy, and White privilege. The problem is that prison postsecondary college educators will most likely be White

NEW DIRECTIONS FOR COMMUNITY COLLEGES • DOI: 10.1002/cc

(Van Gundy, Bryant, & Starks, 2013) and, based upon the historical concerns levied against critical pedogogists, may not have the capacity to reciprocate the learning process by engaging in an ongoing discussion about the nuances of their own socially constructed White privilege. As Woodson (1933) noted in *The Mis-Education of the Negro*, the classroom is where the racial imbalance of power is perpetuated in the psycho-socio framework of the Black American experience.

In reality, the epic journey from humiliation to humility is an extremely difficult one. The road to redemption for an incarcerated Black male returning to his community is paved with temptations, disappointments, and failures. When he goes home, unemployment will still be high. Our educational system will still be broken. He will still have the greatest opportunity to be victimized by a person within his own community of similar race or ethnic background. There will still be more liquor stores than schools in his neighborhood. Street hustlers will still operate in open drug markets with community-supported impunity at times. HHP is a pedagogical approach to help inspire the development of the sole critical factor that can ultimately withstand these warped social and psychological barriers to a successful prison–community transition, and to make the transformation from humiliation to humility: the indestructible nature of the human spirit.

Secondly, the HHP emphasizes that an *Afrocentric* education must be introduced to incarcerated Black males. Incarcerated Black males must become aware of the power of their *cultural survival gene*. For as African scholar Molefi Asante (2003, p. 1) says, "A people without an appreciation of the value of [their] historical experiences will always create chaos." Afrocentricity is defined as "a philosophical perspective associated with the discovery, location, and actualizing of African legacy within the context of history and culture" (Asante, 2003, p. 3). Incarcerated Black males must have the owned knowledge within the Afrocentric paradigm to understand and explain the significance that their ancestral homeland is the birthplace of humanity. Their intellect must be groomed so that they are aware that Africa had a rich economic, religious, and cultural history thousands of years before European colonialism set foot on the continent (Bennett, 1961). Incarcerated Black males must be thoroughly familiar with the fact that the African Holocaust, also commonly known as the transatlantic slave trade, was the single greatest crime ever committed against any people on this planet (Clarke, 1998) and has triggered a chain of culturally destructive social and psychological events that continue to impact the lives of Black Americans today (Anderson, 1999; Dyson, 1996; West, 2001; Wilson, 2009). One need not look any further than to what is occurring in Chicago today to get a clearer picture regarding the cycle of transgenerational trauma facing young Black males (Schwab, 2010). Finally, incarcerated Black males must be able to inspire an "intellectual revolution" among themselves (Gaskew, 2014), one that will resuscitate the culture from the manifest destiny of nihilism long predicted by Du Bois (1994),

Frazier (1968), and Garvey (1986), and that will use the spiritual strength of an education to emancipate the Black American experience from the social and psychological barriers that have kept the culture chained for the 400 years since Jamestown, Virginia.

When I'm volunteering at FCI McKean, it is common to hear incarcerated Black males proudly voice connections to their hometowns of Chicago, Detroit, Philadelphia, Washington, DC, Los Angeles, Atlanta, and the five boroughs of New York City; however, when Africa is mentioned by me it is routinely dismissed with, "I'm an American, born and raised right here … I'm not from the jungle." In fact, I've witnessed more incarcerated Black males proudly voice their loyalty to a gang sect, such as the Black Gangster Disciples, Bloods, or Crips, rather than remotely associate themselves with Africa. Maybe Cureton (2011) makes a valid point regarding his *emergent gangsterism perspective* and its virtual stranglehold on the perpetually lost identities of Black males in America today. You see, today it's the Black diaspora of gangsterism that has convinced Black males that Africa is this primitive land that is only useful when filming a music video, too ignorant to realize that shaming Africa is shaming their own cultural legacy. The "diss Africa campaign" is a phenomenon that is now Black owned, creating a self-inflicted wound on the entire Black community in America. That wound never seems to heal and continues to get worse with time, although the remedy is so obvious: an owned awareness of one's culture and history, an awareness of the only true Black privilege: *Black cultural privilege (BCP)*.

Thirdly, HHP advocates an approach where incarcerated Black males must have a thorough understanding of the criminal justice system. Within the HHP, the goal is to provide incarcerated Black males with access to owned knowledge and a pedagogical formula to deal with the shame of physical servitude, which will improve their "criminal justice system IQ" and help them see the system as both an institutional process and as a business entity: a government sanctioned structural narrative that both criminalizes and profits off the Black American. Incarcerated Black males must understand that the criminal justice system is a carnivorous great white shark with an endless appetite, and that everyone who comes into contact with it is going to be bitten and that their wounds will subsequently become infected. Incarcerated Black males must understand that those who come in contact with the system will either unknowingly or intentionally allow others to swim in shark-infested waters, primarily others of the same race, ethnicity, and class. More importantly, incarcerated Black males will rarely ever again fear the criminal justice system, and will teach the same to their children, family, and community, because they will understand that the only people who have the power to "feed the shark" are themselves.

This is consistent with the fourth HHP principle, knowing the victims. Incarcerated Black males must understand the only true victims of their crimes are their own Black children. At FCI McKean, usually on the very first day of class and toward the end of our allocated two-hour time period, I normally give the students a short sort of "take-home "assignment. I ask them, when they return to their cells, to write down on a piece of paper exactly how much money their lives are worth. When they return the following class, I ask them to write down the monetary figure they either earned or were attempting to earn when they committed their crimes, next to it. Almost 100% of the time, the second monetary figure was significantly lower than what they estimated their lives to be worth. A little laughter follows the discussion because for the first time many of the students realize one thing: how little they value their own lives.

I then ask them to write down the monetary value of their children. I tell them that I want to see an actual figure, and not the typical "my kids are priceless" response. I tell them to compare the monetary value they attached to their children to the monetary value they gave themselves, and to the monetary figure that resulted in their incarceration. Lastly, I tell them that whatever monetary figure they wrote down for their children doesn't even come close to what the market value of their children is to the criminal justice system. I tell them that their children are truly "priceless" to the criminal justice system because it could not sustain itself without them. I tell them "they" as current incarcerated offenders are worth much less to the criminal justice system than their children, because just like purchasing a new car, its value begins to depreciate within 24 hours after bringing it home. I tell them the criminal justice system is always investing in the futures of their children, when no one else seems to care. In the summer of 2013, the City of Philadelphia decided to close 23 public schools, almost 10% of the city's total, which of course would be in areas that disproportionately affect communities of color, while approving the construction of the second most expensive state project ever in Pennsylvania, a new 5,000-bed state-of-the-art $400 million prison complex, Phoenix East and Phoenix West. With a state prison population that is filled with more than 61% Black males, although young Black male adults only represent less than 5% of the Pennsylvania state population, it will not be too difficult predicting who will be filling the majority of the new bed space.

Finally, as Malcolm X said, "In fact, once he is motivated no one can change more completely than the man who has been at the bottom. I call myself the best example of that" (Haley, 1964, p. 261). The HHP emphasizes that once incarcerated Black males begin opening themselves up to owning their truths and the truths of their African history, the criminal justice system, and the importance of caring for the only true victims of their counterculture of crime, their very own children, they now face the most difficult aspect of their journey: to apply this knowledge to make choices in their lives. The first and most important challenge faced by a large portion of incarcerated Black males "intellectually prepared" to finally make choices in their lives is the ability to emancipate themselves from the psychosocial prison "cultural safety cushions."

This is where postsecondary prison education pedagogy becomes such a vital component in the lives of incarcerated Black males. For incarcerated Black males, this is where they begin to subconsciously feel more comfortable in a prison setting than in their own respective Black communities. *Cultural safety cushions* are present in all prison settings from low to high, and normally consist of the following: free meals, free recreation, free medical/health services, no bill collectors, no parenting or family responsibilities, MP3 players, and the continued ability to use violence, intimidation, and gangsterism to foster a Black counterculture of crime. For a young Black male who is already entrenched in the counterculture of crime, whether his prison sentence is 36 or 360 months, the prison setting becomes an extension of the illusion he has already been living outside of the prison walls. Cultural safety cushions are structurally inspired illusions that allow incarcerated Black males to look at their prison setting and feel right at home.

Prison educators can also be a dangerous cultural safety cushion. Many compassionate, dedicated, and decent people walk into prison education settings and try to build an illusion that the "inside" of their classrooms are "outside" of the racism, White supremacy, and White privilege realities that incarcerated Black men must face when they not only leave this educational setting, but more disturbing, when they are released back into their respective communities. The power imbalances created by the social constructs of racism, White supremacy, and White privilege, the same negative forces that contributed to their incarceration, and the same power imbalances that contributed to the success of their prison educators, who are carefully trying to hide this phenomenon by establishing a color-blind learning climate, will be waiting for them with open arms upon their release, and a college education alone will not buffer them from this reality. The overwhelming majority of formerly incarcerated and newly educated Black males will not be the next-door neighbors or work colleagues of their prison educators, despite their academic success inside of a prison college classroom, and these types of discussions must become part of the new pedagogical framework if the ultimate goal of educational programs is to serve the needs of its incarcerated students. The HHP seeks to address these needs.

References

Alexander, M. (2010). *The new Jim Crow: Mass incarceration in the age of colorblindness.* New York, NY: The New Press.
Allen, R. L. (2006). The race problem in the critical pedagogy community. In C. A. Rossatto, R. L. Allen, & M. Pruyn (Eds.), *Reinventing critical pedagogy: Widening the circle of anti-oppression education* (pp. 3–20). Boulder, CO: Rowman & Littlefield Publishers.
American Association of Community Colleges. (2014). *Fast facts from our fact sheet.* Retrieved from http://www.aacc.nche.edu/AboutCC/Pages/fastfactsfactsheet.aspx

NEW DIRECTIONS FOR COMMUNITY COLLEGES • DOI: 10.1002/cc

Anderson, E. (1999). *Code of the street: Decency, violence, and the moral life of the inner city*. New York, NY: W. W. Norton & Company.

Asante, M. (2003). *Afrocentricity: The theory of social change*. Chicago, IL: African American Images.

Bell, D. (1992). *Faces at the bottom of the well*. New York, NY: Basic Books.

Bennett, L. (1961). *Before the Mayflower: A history of Black America*. New York, NY: Penguin Press.

Bonilla-Silva, E. (2005). Racism and new racism: The contours of racial dynamics in contemporary America. In Z. Leonardo (Ed.), *Critical pedagogy and race* (pp. 1–36). Malden, MA: Blackwell Publishing.

Clarke, J. H. (1998). *Christopher Columbus and the African Holocaust: Slavery and the rise of European capitalism*. Hunlock Creek, PA: Eworld Publishing.

Cureton, S. (2011). *Black vanguards and Black gangsters: From seeds of discontent to a declaration of war*. Baltimore, MD: University Press of America.

Davis, L. M., Bozick, R., Steele, J. L., Saunders, J., & Miles, J. M. (2013). *Evaluating the effectiveness of correctional education: A meta-analysis of programs that provide education to incarcerated adults*. The RAND Corporation. Retrieved from https://www.bja .gov/Publications/RAND_Correctional-Education-Meta-Analysis.pdf

Delgado, R., & Stefancic, J. (2005). *The Derrick Bell reader*. New York: New York University Press.

Du Bois, W. E. B. (1994). *The souls of Black folk*. New York, NY: Dover Publications.

Dyson, M. (1996). *Race rules: Navigating the color line*. New York, NY: Vintage Books.

Forbes, C., & Kaufman, P. (2008). Critical pedagogy in the sociology classrooms: Challenges and concerns. *Teaching Sociology, 36*, 26–33.

Foster, M. (1997). *Black teachers on teaching*. New York, NY: New Press.

Frazier, F. E. (1968). *Race relations*. Chicago, IL: The University of Chicago Press.

Garvey, A. J. (1986). *Philosophy and opinions of Marcus Garvey*. Dover, MA: Majority Press.

Gaskew, T. (2014). *Rethinking prison reentry: Transforming humiliation into humility*. Lanham, MD: Lexington Books.

Haley, A. (1964). *The autobiography of Malcolm X*. Westminster, MD: Ballantine.

hooks, b. (2003). *Teaching community: A pedagogy of hope*. New York, NY: Routledge.

Irvine, J. J. (1988). An analysis of the problem of the disappearing Black educators. *Elementary School Journal, 88*(5), 503–513.

Irvine, J. J. (1990). *Black students and school failure: Policies, practices, and prescriptions*. Westport, CT: Greenwood Press.

Leonardo, Z. (Ed.). (2005). *Critical pedagogy and race*. Malden, MA: Blackwell Publishing.

Lynn, M. (1999). Toward a critical race pedagogy: A research note. *Urban Education, 33*(5), 606–626.

Lynn, M. (2005). Critical race theory, Afrocentricity, and their relationship to critical pedagogy. In Z. Leonardo (Ed.), *Critical pedagogy and race* (pp. 127–139). Malden, MA: Blackwell Publishing.

National Center for Education Statistics. (2014). Table 264. Total fall enrollment in degree-granting institutions, by level and control of institution and race/ethnicity of student: Selected years, 1976 through 2011. *Digest of education statistics*. Retrieved from http://nces.ed.gov/programs/digest/d12/tables/dt12_264.asp

Rossatto, C. A., Allen, R. L., & Pruyn, M. (Eds.). (2006). *Reinventing critical pedagogy: Widening the circle of anti-oppression education*. Boulder, CO: Rowman & Littlefield Publishers.

Ryan, T. A., & McCabe, K. A. (1994). Mandatory versus voluntary prison education and academic achievement. *The Prison Journal, 74*, 450–461.

Schwab, G. (2010). *Haunting legacies: Violent histories and transgenerational trauma*. New York, NY: Columbia University Press.

Van Gundy, A., Bryant, A., & Starks, B. C. (2013). Pushing the envelope for evolution and social change: Critical challenges for teaching inside-out. *The Prison Journal*, *93*(2), 189–210.

West, C. (2001). *Race matters*. Boston, MA: Vintage Press.

West, H. C., Sabol, W. J., & Greenman, S. J. (2011). *Prisoners in 2009*. U.S. Department of Justice, Office of Justice Programs, Bureau of Justice Statistics. Retrieved from http://www.bjs.gov/content/pub/pdf/p09.pdf

Wilson, J. (2009). *More than just race: Being Black and poor in the inner city*. New York, NY: W. W. Norton and Company.

Woodson, C. G. (1933). *The mis-education of the negro*. New York, NY: Tribeca Books.

TONY GASKEW *is an associate professor of criminal justice and the director of the Criminal Justice Program at the University of Pittsburgh (Bradford).*

NEW DIRECTIONS FOR COMMUNITY COLLEGES • DOI: 10.1002/cc

8

In this chapter, the author describes her experience teaching in a women's prison in New York, the challenges that arose with teaching autobiography, and the distinct situation of women behind bars.

Teaching Academic Writing in a Maximum Security Women's Prison

Jane Maher

People ask me all the time what it's like to teach in a women's prison, and I usually just say it's pretty much the same as teaching on the "outside." I give this answer because more often than not, the people who ask are far more interested in the prison itself, the Bedford Hills Correctional Facility for Women in Westchester County, New York, rather than the teaching. Is it safe? What crimes did the inmates commit? Does an officer guard you in the classroom? And most recently, "Do you watch *Orange Is the New Black*?" People are also somewhat fascinated by the notoriety of some of the women who have served time at Bedford. Here in New York, I can tell a person's age by whether he or she asks me about Jean Harris (older than 55), Amy Fisher (between 25 and 40), or Martha Stewart (all ages, but Stewart was in a federal prison in Virginia). And given that I am in academia, I still encounter many 1960s radicals who remember the Weather Underground and ask about Kathy Boudin (she has been released) and Judy Clark (she has not been released). It is not that I am impatient or that I don't want to talk about the prison; it is that I find it impossible to simplify or condense the complexity of teaching in a maximum security prison for women, and I sense that people don't really want to hear about the teaching as much as the place and the inmates.

The readers of this chapter, however, *are* interested in the pedagogical, and therefore my purpose is to explain and describe the way my teaching has evolved over the 16 years I have been teaching at Bedford. Although there *are* many similarities between teaching in a maximum security prison and teaching on the outside, there are crucial differences that must be recognized and addressed, and as I became aware of them, I believe that the teaching and learning occurring in my prison classes improved.

NEW DIRECTIONS FOR COMMUNITY COLLEGES, no. 170, Summer 2015 © 2015 Wiley Periodicals, Inc.
Published online in Wiley Online Library (wileyonlinelibrary.com) • DOI: 10.1002/cc.20146

I have been teaching pre-college and college-level writing courses, together with upper-level literature and survey courses, at the Bedford Hills Correctional Facility for Women since 1998, and I have been teaching composition (primarily remedial and first-year writing courses) at Nassau Community College on Long Island, New York, for 35 years, where I am currently a full-time, tenured professor. For a long while I actually believed that unless I concentrated on the similarities between teaching on the "outside" and on the "inside" (these are terms that are commonly used by both prisoners and civilians), I would not be an effective teacher for the women at Bedford. It took some time (and mistakes) for me to realize that unless I acknowledged and addressed the differences, teaching in prison was not going to go well for me or for my students. I don't just mean the differences caused by the prison environment, although they are substantial: the security protocols that seem to change arbitrarily depending on which officer is on duty; the background checks and fingerprinting and annual tuberculosis testing; the rules and regulations about what and who can go in and out and when this can occur; the automatic gates and concertina wire and hand stamping and searching of belongings and head counts; the lack of the most basic necessities such as copy and fax machines; the inability to e-mail students; the inability to look something up on the Internet during a class conversation; the inability to lend a pen to a student if she has forgotten hers, because the pen has a spring in it. And don't even think about Smart Boards. In the past five years, I have been compensating for the fact that more and more of my students on the outside do not know how to read cursive by using Google Docs to provide comments, suggestions, and assessment. However, when I grade the writing assignments of the women at Bedford, 70% of whom cannot read cursive, I have to remind myself, over and over again, to print my comments. This seems like a small enough inconvenience, but with 20 women in a writing class, it can take an extra hour, maybe two. Although these circumstances make teaching somewhat harder, they can be offset by careful and thoughtful advance planning.

It is the differences in the students that can sidetrack a teacher in a prison setting, particularly a prison like Bedford Hills, where many of the women are serving long sentences for pretty serious crimes. There's the danger of romanticizing the situation: These women are victims of a system, of society, of class, of race, of culture. And it's true to an enormous extent; everyone knows we imprison too many people in this country for crimes that could have been prevented with intervention or that would be better addressed through treatment rather than incarceration. However, this attitude can lead to sentimentality, and the last thing in the world any student needs, particularly one who is trying to earn a college degree so that she can have some small chance of finding employment when she is released, is a sentimental instructor. But there's also the danger of thinking about what the students did to wind up in the only maximum security prison for women in New York State. Because I pretty much only read the *New York Times*, I

NEW DIRECTIONS FOR COMMUNITY COLLEGES • DOI: 10.1002/cc

tend to know relatively little about the more lurid and sensational crimes being committed in New York, but occasionally I will hear something on the radio or notice a headline in the *Post* or the *Daily News*, and I realize that if a female has been convicted (a boyfriend is often convicted as well), she will probably be at Bedford in about a year and may very well enroll in the college program. It's just a passing thought, but it's there.

The students at Bedford are somewhat stronger writers than my community college students; this may be because they write so many letters to family and friends, to lawyers, to judges, to case workers, to child protective services agencies, to politicians, given that they have limited access to phones and no access to the Internet. However, the same writing issues still need to be addressed to prepare the students for the kind of writing that is expected of them, particularly in upper-level courses: generating ideas, organizing information, identifying and incorporating evidence, eliminating errors in grammar and usage.

But no one would ever confuse Bedford for a college campus. It is a huge and old facility, and it always seems dirty and run down despite the fact that the women's work assignments include constantly scraping and painting walls and gates and cleaning and polishing the worn linoleum floors. But there is also the unexpected and wonderful presence of very young children and puppies—Bedford is one of the few prisons in the United States in which women are permitted to keep their infant children with them in a nursery unit, and there is a thriving program through which inmates raise and train the puppies who will eventually go on to become assistance dogs for the disabled.

There are approximately 800 inmates at Bedford, and almost 200 of them are in our pre-college and college program. Eighty percent of our students are women of color, and 90% of them attended school in New York City. A closer analysis of the schools they attended shows that an enormous majority of our students come from school districts with the lowest reading scores in New York State, thus the need for our pre-college program. Many women arrive at Bedford without a high school diploma and earn their GEDs in prison. The number of inmates with mental illness is increasing each year at Bedford, a reflection of New York State's lack of facilities or treatment centers for this population. Many of our students are on what everyone in the prison refers to as "mental meds." Occasionally, a student will submit an essay that is incomprehensible one week and an essay that is perfectly cogent the next, and those of us who have been teaching at the prison long enough to understand this just ask the student to rewrite her essay, hoping that she won't skip too many more medication lines before the end of the semester.

These statistics are not very different than those of most urban community, two-year colleges. My students on the outside are from some of the same school districts as the women at Bedford; some of them suffer from mental illness, and they are often juggling family and work responsibilities, making it very difficult for them to thrive in college. The women at Bedford must work as well. The idea that prisoners have a lot of time and nothing to do is truly ludicrous: Their schedules are so tightly regimented with mandatory work assignments and programs that even our best students cannot handle more than two college courses per semester. And our students at Bedford juggle family responsibilities as well—they even have a program called "Parenting from the Inside" to help the women develop and maintain healthy relationships with their children, who are often being cared for by aging and financially strapped grandparents, usually grandmothers. There is an expression that I've heard a lot to describe the family dynamics of prisoners: When a man goes to prison, his wife or the mother of his children takes care of things at home. When a woman goes to prison, there goes the home.

The similarities between my students on the outside and on the inside served me well when I began my work at Bedford; my learning curve was far less steep than it was (and is) for professors and tutors who do not come from a community college environment. The same theorists who guide me on the outside—Mike Rose, Mina Shaughnessy (whose biography I wrote), Jonathan Kozol, Lisa Delpit, Marilyn Sternglass, Shirley Brice Heath, Pedro Noguera—guide my teaching on the inside as well. However, I knew from the moment I read the first set of essays from my students at Bedford that I would not be able to use the same writing assignments or topics. Autobiographical writing from my students on the outside often provides me with crucial information that I can use to design reading and writing assignments that will engage them. Of course, my students on the outside (some of whom are veterans of Afghanistan and Iraq) experience the same challenges and frustrations that all first-generation college students face, and these struggles continue to be exacerbated by the fact that the recession does not seem to have ended for my students. However, I was simply not prepared for the autobiographical writing that my students at Bedford submitted.

When I first began teaching at Bedford, I usually started with a somewhat autobiographical topic simply to give the students a chance to write about what was familiar to them. These were not tell-me-about-your-life topics—I was not that naïve; rather they were intended to reflect and prepare the students for the general theme/readings of the course: education, immigration, poverty in the United States, gender issues (pre-college and lower-level courses); African-American women's contributions to the Civil Rights Movement, the northern migration, the Harlem Renaissance, the Native American experience (upper-level courses). However, in the lower-level courses in particular, the students would describe events or scenes that were so difficult to read I would be unable to function as an instructor. Try pointing out a run-on sentence or ask for clarifying details in an essay that described a scene in the prison visiting room during which an 11-year-old daughter asked her mother, who has a life sentence, what would become of her body when she died in prison. Or the student who recalled staying late after school every day so she would not have to arrive home before her aunt; if she did, her aunt's boyfriend would sexually molest her and threaten to kill her puppy if she told. Or the student who described the birth of her son in painstakingly precise detail (I know, this happens on the outside as well), but then fast-forwarded 10 years to explain she had recently received an official notification from Child Protective Services saying her child was being removed from a foster home because he had been physically and sexually abused. "I can't concentrate tonight as I write this essay for class because I don't know where my son is at and I don't know if he is hurt bad." Some of these essays would end with detailed explanations of being imprisoned unfairly, descriptions of poor legal representation, accounts of the appeals the students are currently working on for reduced sentences or clemency. Often there would be a request for me to write a letter of support, although I had only met the student one or two times. (I say no to all such requests. This may seem harsh, but the rules governing what a volunteer can write and to whom are so difficult to understand, much less follow, that I have decided I am of sufficient value to the women as a professor that I will not jeopardize my volunteer status by inadvertently breaking rules.)

When I first started teaching at Bedford, I would try to do what I always do on the outside early in the semester: type a few sentences or a paragraph from each student's first draft in order to create a "text" from which we could discuss and learn about whatever skill needed to be addressed. The excerpts from my classes on the outside often consist of sentences or paragraphs that reflect the struggles of first-generation college students—unemployment, the loss of a parent, even homelessness. However, my first samples from Bedford would have read like a collection of headlines from the *National Enquirer* if I hadn't chosen the most innocuous sentences—usually from the beginning of the essay. As a result, the worksheets were useless and boring. And of course there was the issue of privacy; my students at Bedford would share information in their essays that they should only have shared with a (trusted) counselor—descriptions that would keep me awake at night—yet if I even mentioned in class one innocuous detail from the most recent set of essays in order to make a point, I would get a self-stick note stuck to my desk within 30 seconds telling me I had betrayed a sacred trust.

And so I began to avoid the autobiographical entirely, at least in the lower-level courses. Instead, I chose texts that contained characters and experiences and events to which the women could relate, and I asked them to analyze and compare events or processes or characters or circumstances. I used excerpts but more often I used complete texts: Richard Wright's (1993) *Black Boy* paired with James McBride's (1996) *The Color of Water*; Sonia Nazario's (2007) *Enrique's Journey* paired with Kien Nguyen's (2001) *The Unwanted*; Jimmy Santiago Baca's (2001) *A Place to Stand* read together with J. R. Moehringer's (2006) *The Tender Bar*. I thought the women would like Jeannette Walls's (2005) *The Glass Castle*, but they struggled with it. One of the women said that Walls didn't seem to know how bad her life was. When I noted that the entire book was pretty much about how bad Walls's life was, my student did her best to help me understand what she meant. "You just don't write all that stuff for other people to read," she explained. I nodded as if I understood, stopped myself from delivering a lecture about the purpose of memoir, and resolved to think far more carefully about the content and style of the book before I used it again at Bedford.

While my students were engaged in these texts and were able to write about them in the academic way I wanted, I also began to realize that I was choosing books that had, for lack of a better term, "happy" endings. Even though every character suffered in these memoirs, they had prevailed. I began to realize why my students' autobiographical writing was so problematic. They were, given the fact that they were in prison, at what was probably the worst time/point of their lives. If the lives of the students at Bedford are going to end "happily," they don't know it yet, at least not for certain. They lacked the distance that is essential for reflection, analysis, and understanding. I used more sociological books for my 200-level courses, and I had to laugh when the women remained suspicious of Barbara Ehrenreich (2001) as she toiled away at minimum-wage jobs in order to write *Nickel and Dimed.* "She may have gotten down on all fours to clean a bathroom floor," one of the students wrote in a reflection, "but all the while, she had that credit card in her back pocket and she could use it when the going got too rough."

When David Margolick's (2011) *Elizabeth and Hazel: Two Women of Little Rock* was published, it segued perfectly with our reading of Melba Patillo Beals's (1994) *Warriors Don't Cry.* As we compared and contrasted Elizabeth and Hazel, one White, one Black; one tormented, the other the tormentor; one ready to be forgiven, the other unable to forgive, I realized the women were able to insert themselves into the conversation and use their experiences as written evidence or as illustration of a point of view. The book was published in 2011; by then I had been teaching at Bedford for 13 years. I remember wondering if perhaps the women had always been capable of including themselves and their experiences; maybe I just needed all that time to figure out how to provide the opportunity for them to do it. It was at about this time that I read an essay by Mike Rose (2012) entitled "Rethinking Remedial Education and the Academic-Vocational Divide." I realized he was describing my students on the inside as well as the outside when he complained about the lack of "close analysis of what goes on in classrooms. ... We don't get much of a sense of the texture of students' lives ... [and] even less of a sense of the power of learning new things and through that learning redefining who you are" (p. 12). I had finally figured how to make it possible for the students at Bedford to redefine who they were through "learning new things," through reading. My students on the outside balk when I assign entire books; in fact, I often can't even get them to purchase the books in the first place. The women at Bedford, however, would often come to class having read the entire book even though I had only assigned 100 or 200 pages. They would laugh when I would explain that *I* had followed the syllabus and only (re)read up the assigned page and thus they would have to direct the conversation.

As the women gain more academic experience and confidence as students, as intellectuals, they begin to master the way the personal can be used to explicate a theme or theory. An example of this is an assignment from my Harlem Renaissance course in which I asked the students to replace the narrator's voice in Langston Hughes's (1951) "Theme from English B" with their own. The results reflected the students' ability to interpret the poem, of course, and it allowed them to examine their own educational journeys within parameters that seemed to serve both the assignment and their need for self-expression. A student who asked not to be identified gave me permission to share her poem:

How to Be Free
Professor Jane said something that filled me with fright
"Besides *all* your homework, you must write a poem tonight.
Let it come from you and let it be true."
What an instruction! What shall I do?
I live in New York but am from Trinidad
Then I came to Bedford Hills and I was pretty sad.
I said "Let me do the right thing, college ain't that bad."
It connects me to the world, for that I can't be sad.
New York I hear you! Let us talk on this page.
Let me write about my love, joy, passion, and rage.
Let me speak to you about my five years in this cage
Let me free my conscience from this injustice and pain.
I like to eat, sleep, dance and enjoy life
I like Biggie, Bach, Beethoven and jazz if it's light. That's right!
I might be locked up but I'm no different from other people
I'm not defined by the lenses other people see through.
The message of this poem won't be incarcerated when I write
In fact it's free as my words leave prison on this page tonight.
They will linger in your mind creating rays of light.
As I learned from you, instructor, you learn from me
I am incarcerated yes, but my words set me free!

I think back to an incident that occurred very early in my tenure at Bedford, when I was administering the pre-college program. One of the counselors insisted that I come to her office where she reprimanded me for allowing another instructor to show *The Sweet Hereafter*—a movie about incest that had caused one of the students to return to her unit and cut herself up so badly she needed to be taken to an outside hospital. Did any of us White, middle-class professors even know what cutting was at that time?

As educators, we often ask ourselves how long it will take for our students to develop the skills they need to be successful, but if we are going to teach in a prison, it is imperative to ask ourselves how long it will take for us to develop the skills we need to be successful as teachers of this extraordinarily complex and demanding population of students.

Even after all these years, I still make mistakes at Bedford: writing comments that are too heavy handed and do little to make the students want to write more and better; overplanning to compensate for the short amount of time we have together each week; insisting that the students work in groups even after they remind me, time and time again, that they eat, sleep, shower, work, and pray together. Can't they at least, as one of the women asked, "Have my own space to learn?" I lost my patience last semester when every one of my 21 students crowded around me during the break to complain about a grade, to ask me to repeat an assignment, to request material from the Internet, to explain why yet another homework assignment was going to be late. As I drive home from class each week, tired and anxious because I have yet to prepare for the next day's classes on the outside, I think of what I could have done differently, how I could have reacted more calmly, been more supportive. I have the same issues with my students on the outside, of course, but I can send them an e-mail or a text, ask them to come to my office. And my students on the outside don't take me so seriously—college is only one part of their very busy lives. At Bedford, college is, as one of my students wrote, "the only thing that keeps me alive."

Keeping our college program alive is something that concerns all of us, all of the time. Marymount Manhattan College, led by President Judson Shaver, provides everything we need, but it must fundraise to pay for the program and answer to those who do not believe a prison "satellite campus" is a good use of its resources. Our on-site academic director, Aileen Baumgartner, works endlessly to balance academic requirements with correctional ones—a recent memo reminded us about both grade inflation and gate clearances. Those of us who believe that college is a good thing for the women—and studies have shown that the recidivism rate decreases as the level of college education for inmates increases—rejoiced when New York's Governor Andrew Cuomo proposed that college programs be expanded in New York State prisons, with public funds covering the cost. However, scores of politicians derided his proposal, foremost among them Rob Astorino, who opposed Cuomo in the New York gubernatorial election. In a public speech delivered days after Cuomo's proposal, Astorino declared that he was going to sit his 10-year-old son down and explain to him that he was "on a new career track." Instead of putting money into his three kids' 529 plans, Astorino explained, to laughter and applause from his audience, "I told my son yesterday that when he turns 18, 'you're going to rob that bank in Poughkeepsie so you can have a free ride in college.'" Would it do any good to explain to Astorino that not one of my students this semester even knows what a 529 plan is? That in fact most of my students at Bedford this semester do not know who either one or both of their parents are? That maybe if we provided a better education to prisoners either before they are incarcerated or while they are incarcerated, some day maybe they can start 529 plans for their own children?

Something all teachers in prisons must remember (although so many of our politicians don't seem to get this) is that an overwhelming majority of our students will eventually be released. When they return to the outside, the quality of the education they received in prison will be the only thing they have to offset the fact that they will have to check the *yes* box on the application next to the question "Have you ever been incarcerated?" Both teachers and students in a prison setting must work harder because the stakes are so much higher. Given that I have been teaching at the prison for such a long time, I am now able to see the results of our efforts. Many of our students have earned their degrees, and many of them have been released and are succeeding in their careers. I hear from former students all the time, and I am heartened when they tell me that they are making it on the outside as a result of the college degrees they earned while in prison.

Recently, I received an e-mail with an attachment from a former Bedford inmate who had earned her bachelor's degree. She asked me to review a memo she had written for her supervisors at a foundation that serves ex-offenders. "I used to hate your comments and corrections on my drafts," she wrote, "but now I'm glad you were so tough. Let loose with your red pen on this one; it's going to the big suits in the company." I didn't have to let loose; I only had to make a few tracked changes (and I intentionally chose the color blue). The memo was clear and articulate and convincing. As good, maybe even better, than anything my students on the outside could have written.

References

Baca, J. S. (2001). *A place to stand: The making of a poet.* New York, NY: Grove Press.

Beals, M. P. (1994). *Warriors don't cry.* New York, NY: Washington Square Press.

Ehrenreich, B. (2001). *Nickel and dimed: On (not) getting by in America.* New York, NY: Henry Holt.

Hughes, L. (1951). "Theme for English B". Retrieved from http://www.eecs.harvard.edu/~keith/poems/English_B.html

Margolick, D. (2011). *Elizabeth and Hazel: Two women of Little Rock.* New Haven, CT: Yale University Press.

McBride, J. (1996). *The color of water: A Black man's tribute to his White mother.* New York, NY: Riverhead Books.

Moehringer, J. R. (2006). *The tender bar.* New York, NY: Hyperion.

Nazario, S. (2007). *Enrique's journey.* New York, NY: Random House.

Nguyen, K. (2001). *The unwanted: A memoir of childhood.* Boston, MA: Little Brown and Company.

Rose, M. (2012). Rethinking remedial education and the academic-vocational divide. *Mind, Culture, and Activity, 19*(1), 1–16.
Walls, J. (2005). *The glass castle.* New York, NY: Simon & Schuster.
Wright, R. (1993). *Black boy.* New York, NY: Harper Collins.

Jane Maher is a professor of writing at Nassau Community College and coordinator of special programs in the college program at the Bedford Hill Correctional Facility for Women in Westchester County, New York.

9

This chapter describes the contribution of art education to the wider project of prison education, and posits a "natural partnership" between prison arts and community college programs in prisons.

Prison Fine Arts and Community College Programs: A Partnership to Advance Inmates' Life Skills

Larry Brewster

Leon is an excellent example of an inmate who chose to take a different path by way of the California Arts-in-Corrections program, which in turn gave him the confidence to complete his GED and enroll in college courses. At an early age, Leon expected to end up in prison, as had his father, two uncles, and so many other Black brothers from his south Los Angeles 'hood. He not only expected to go to prison, but looked forward to it. He romanticized prison as a place where real men earned their badges of courage and respect. His role models served time, and it was expected that he would do the same. He did. Leon served more than 20 years, during which he eventually decided he wanted a better life for himself and his seven children.

Leon started reading on his own and then enrolled in Arts-in-Corrections, a fine arts program. Through the program he discovered his talents as a songwriter, playwright, actor, and painter. His arts education and practice also gave him the work ethic, discipline, and confidence to earn his GED and pursue a college education. Since his release nearly six years ago, he has completed a novel and cowritten and acted in a play. He continues to write, paint, and play music while working a full-time job to support his wife and children. In our interview, Leon spoke with great passion about the satisfaction he receives from completing projects and the importance of teaching his children that they too can do anything they set their minds to, as long as they are willing to work hard and especially complete what they start. In his words,

> The combination of the arts program and college education taught me above all else the importance of completing projects. I think one of the problems with young people today is that they don't finish what they start. They may

NEW DIRECTIONS FOR COMMUNITY COLLEGES, no. 170, Summer 2015 © 2015 Wiley Periodicals, Inc.
Published online in Wiley Online Library (wileyonlinelibrary.com) • DOI: 10.1002/cc.20147

get interested in something but often don't follow through. I was like that
for most of my life. But not anymore. I've learned with the help of others,
especially my teachers, how satisfying it is to complete tasks and get better at
my writing in the process. (Interview with Leon, October 3, 2010)

The irony for Leon, and so many others like him, is that for the first
time in their lives prison provides the opportunity to reflect on why they are
so self-destructive and to question what they can do to change their lives for
the better. A common refrain heard over and over again when interviewing
incarcerated and formerly incarcerated men and women who were involved
in prison arts education was that the arts program helped to light a spark of
self-worth and served as a gateway and catalyst in pursuit of other academic
or vocational programs (Brewster, 2014).

Educating the whole person is achieved in a learning environment that
integrates rigorous inquiry, creative imagination, and reflective engagement
within self and society. This goal is ever more critical in an age with a growing education and achievement gap in preparing people, including prisoners, for employment and a meaningful life. Community colleges especially play an ever-more-important role in preparing the incarcerated for
employment by offering academic and vocational programs inside the walls.
Community colleges are uniquely positioned for this role considering their
mission to serve the greater community through open access admission and
their close proximity to prisons. A 2005 study by the Institute for Higher Education Policy reported in a 50-state analysis that 68% of all postsecondary
correctional education is provided by community colleges.

In addition to the growing number of community college prison programs, there are fine arts programs in at least 41 state correctional systems,
as well as in many federal prisons. Art programs for inmates are becoming
more common, and research provides compelling evidence that the arts can
and do serve as champions of change in learning. Prison fine arts programs
provide incarcerated men and women with authentic learning experiences
that engage their minds and hearts. Arts education and practice involve
multiple skills and abilities and nurture the development of cognitive, personal, and social competencies (Brewster, 2014; Langelid, Maki, Raundrup,
& Svensson, 2009). Further, fine arts prison programs act to heal and bring
communities together.

The Intersection of Prison Arts and Academic Programs

The growth of prison-based community college academic and vocation programs, as well as fine arts instruction are critical steps in the direction
of preparing inmates for life after prison. Further, these programs help to
relieve tension and improve inmate behavior while incarcerated. Unfortunately, these programs most often are administered separately, with little or
no coordination or integration of curriculum. Prison arts programs, usually

classified as leisure-time activities, do not earn college credits even though many classes are taught by professional artist-teachers who have MFA or other academic degrees. On the other hand, community colleges offer for-credit, degree-granting, and vocation certificate programs.

We argue in this paper that a partnership between community college and arts education prison programs would enhance academic offerings, motivate and better prepare inmates for their educational journey, improve program efficiency and administrative support, and help to justify additional funding. Interdisciplinary research supports the idea of marrying arts education and practice with other academic disciplines. Studies show that training in the arts can improve academic performance; motivate students to complete their education (Brewster, 2012a; Jiang & Winfree, 2006; Silber, 2005); enhance interpersonal, critical thinking, and verbal skills (Langelid et al., 2009; Winner & Hetland, 2007); and provide a safe and acceptable way to express, release, and deal with potentially destructive feelings such as anger and aggression (Blacker, Watson, & Beech, 2008), which helps to reduce the number and severity of disciplinary actions.

Creativity, self-expression, and a greater sense of self-worth and competence are also important outcomes of art learning (Sautter, 1994; Stevens, 2000). Equally important, art is a form of work. Through art, inmates like Leon learn the meaning and joy of work, especially high-quality work that challenges them to do their very best for its own sake. Work is one of the noblest expressions of the human spirit, and art is the visible evidence of work carried to the highest level (Directorate General for Education and Culture, European Commission, 2011).

A recent quantitative evaluation of California Arts-in-Corrections courses, as well as actor and director Tim Robbins's Actors' Gang prison project (offering theater workshops), confirmed the findings of other research, showing a statistically significant correlation between arts education and the motivation to successfully pursue other educational opportunities in prison. Further, those who had participated in the long-running Arts-in-Corrections program compared with those who were untrained in the arts showed significant improvement in behavior as well as better time management, self-confidence, greater intellectual flexibility, social competence, achievement motivation, and emotional control, as measured through the nationally tested "Life Effectiveness Questionnaire." We also found that inmates who had participated in the program for two or more years were far more likely to complete their GED, earn an associate's degree, and/or acquire vocational training and certification than were those inmates surveyed who were untrained in the arts (Brewster, 2014).

Prison Arts Programs

Prisoners have expressed themselves in writing, poetry, music, drawing, painting and other art forms for as long as men and women have been locked up. Prison arts programs offer inmates the opportunity to study and practice their art with the guidance of professional artists and the necessary supplies and equipment. The American painter Robert Henri believed each of us desires to create, to be creative. Art and life, he wrote, are tightly intertwined, and given the opportunity and encouragement, the "art spirit" in each of us can be unleashed, freeing us to become "an inventive, searching, daring, self-expressing creature" (Henri, 2007, p. 11). He understood that the creative life is a desirable one and is possible for every person who is willing to work at it.

The artistic process is one path to an understanding of self and our world. We know, for example, that art as part of a general education program enables students to perform better in all their other subjects. Why? Because they discover that there is an inner voice with which they can speak. They show us themselves in a positive way, giving pleasure and gaining self-awareness. They also learn something as simple and profound as discipline. By doing something over and again, you become better at it, whether you are trying to learn where to put your fingers on a keyboard for a C-sharp minor scale or trying to master the history of the United States (Sautter, 1994).

Prison arts programs take many forms, with some specializing in theater, music, or creative writing, while many other programs offer a comprehensive selection of fine arts instruction. The granddaddy of modern prison arts programming, and a model for many programs across the country, is the California Arts-in-Corrections, founded in 1977 and closed in 2010—a victim of the Great Recession and California's budget crisis. Now that better times have returned to the Golden State, and based on the findings of recently completed program evaluations, the Department of Corrections and Rehabilitation announced on May 3, 2014 that $1 million would be awarded to prison arts programs for the remainder of this fiscal year, and an additional $1.5 million would be awarded in the 2014–2015 fiscal year. The funds will support theater, music, visual arts, and creative writing programs offered by the William James Association, The Actors' Gang (under the direction of Academy Award–winning actor and director Tim Robbins), the Marin Shakespeare Company, and other arts organizations.

Eloise Smith, the inspiration and architect of Arts-in-Corrections, wanted to

> . . . provide an opportunity where a man [or woman] can gain the satisfaction of creation rather than destruction, earn the respect of his [or her] fellows, and gain recognition and appreciation from family and outsiders . . . provide the professional artist as a model of creative self-discipline, and show the making of art as work which demands quality, commitment, and patience. (Brewster, 2012b, p. 2–3)

The program was state funded and included a program manager and full-time civil service artist-facilitators who were located at each of the prisons. Artist-facilitators were responsible for recruiting, supervising, and evaluating artist-instructors, enrolling and monitoring inmates, scheduling classes, and purchasing art supplies, as well as navigating the prison bureaucracy and its complex and ever-changing rules and regulations. The facilitators became the first resident artists to be hired under California's civil service system.

Arts-in-Corrections provided inmates with instruction and mentoring in the performing arts as well as in the visual, literary, and fine craft disciplines. An important goal of the program was to provide inmates with a constructive leisure-time activity to help relieve tensions created by confinement, spur the passage of time, and promote the physical and mental health of inmates. Artist facilitators and instructors had to be trained, active, and successful artists who, it was believed, would most benefit inmates as mentors and inspirational role models. Professional artists shared with inmates through their own experience the demands of the artistic process and the hard work and self-discipline required of artists.

Eloise Smith believed that the artistic process could provide inmates with heightened opportunities for problem-solving, developing self-discipline, exercising impulse control, and improving confidence and self-esteem—all important building blocks in preparing inmates for life after prison. Arts-in-Corrections offered a unique and bold approach to prison arts programming and served as the standard bearer for programs elsewhere.

Wayne Kramer, cofounder of Jail Guitar Doors and a highly respected guitarist and songwriter, provides inmates with donated Fender guitars and offers music workshops as payback for the time he served in federal prison for possession of drugs in the early 1970s. He knows the power of art—music in his case—while doing time. In his words,

> A change of heart is what art, music, writing, theater, painting, sculpture, poetry and dance can produce, leading to a fundamental change in the way an offender sees himself. Art is anger management. I know from my years in prison that prison is a world designed to reinforce the feeling that you are worthless. Being able to create something where there was nothing is a great argument against that worthlessness. The self-discipline required to create a song teaches the songwriter that change is possible. Something from nothing. That you can make it in the world. (Hearing of the Joint Committee on the Arts, 2013)

Just as in community colleges, arts programs in prison can be a public expression of a higher education community, allowing students to share their vision and work with others, making it possible for the entire prison population to benefit and be inspired by those who choose to use their incarceration as an opportunity for growth and change. This model for self-improvement exists in stark contrast to the lowest common denominator—tough guys, gang grouping, and an antiauthoritarian ethos that restrains personal growth.

Community College and Prison Arts Programs: A Natural Partnership

The ultimate goal of a partnership between prison arts and community college academic programs is to provide intellectually stimulating educational experiences that foster human connection, an appreciation for the arts, and resources for positive self-expression and personal growth. It is assumed that such a collaboration will be an evolutionary and dynamic process fueled by a dedicated group of artists, writers, and scholars who believe that knowledge and creative development can be a life-changing experience. Four conditions that promote the partnerships were identified in a U.S. Department of Education study. They are: affordability as compared with other higher education institutions, geographical distribution of community colleges placing them in close proximity to prisons, institutional accreditation, and the mission of open access (Office of Vocational and Adult Education, 2009). We also believe the partnerships will yield administrative and fiscal benefits in support of both programs.

Recruiting New and Motivated Students.   Prison arts programs are fertile ground for preparing and then recruiting inmates into community college academic programs. It is reasonable to assume that many more inmate-artists would enroll in community college courses if they were given at least some college credits for their art classes. It is understood that this requires an evaluation of artist-teachers and their courses to determine if they are worthy of college credits—a process facilitated by a formal partnership agreement. Ideally, the community college and prison arts programs would share responsibility in planning, marketing, and scheduling, with final evaluation of academic quality by the college administration.

We know from prison arts program evaluations that most artist-teachers are academically trained, professional artists who teach outside of prison and who often favorably compare inmate students with their other students. They tell us that most inmates demonstrate a greater appreciation for education than the average student, and almost always come to class prepared and motivated to learn. Multidisciplinary research confirms that arts education serves to attract and enable incarcerated students who have experienced little academic success and may otherwise be reluctant to participate in educational programs (Clements, 2004; Gussak & Ploumis-Devick, 2004).

Proposed Program of Study.   The ultimate goal of a partnership between prison arts and community college programs is for inmates to complete their associate's degree and eventually their bachelor's degree. A logical course of study for these inmates might well be an associate of arts in general studies, or a liberal arts degree with an arts and humanities emphasis.

NEW DIRECTIONS FOR COMMUNITY COLLEGES • DOI: 10.1002/cc

The program could include courses in English (prison arts programs often include creative writing and poetry courses), humanities, and art history. The combined programs would strive to prepare students with academic skills and methods of critical analysis that will help them negotiate some of the tensions that shape their everyday existence; expand their personal horizons; structure professional ambitions; and prepare them to join the workforce as informed citizens. These degree programs are also designed to satisfy the core curriculum for most bachelor's degrees.

Shared Administrative Responsibilities.   Very often prison arts and community college academic programs are understaffed and underfunded. We believe a partnership will facilitate sharing staff and jointly pursuing additional state and foundation funding. Prison arts programs usually are run by nonprofit organizations consisting of paid and volunteer staff. Artist-teachers are usually paid hourly or a per-course stipend. Most community college prison programs are overseen by full-time staff and faculty. While we do not propose a formal, contractual blending of staff and faculty, we do think there are opportunities for staff and faculty in both programs to assist one another in navigating the labyrinth of rules and procedures that define prison life.

Although there are many different models for delivering prison arts programming, an ideal approach for the type of partnership we are proposing is that of the California Arts-in-Corrections program. Arts-in-Corrections employed civil service staff (the first prison arts program in the country to do so) in the role of director, and artist-facilitators (in some programs they are called lead artist-teachers) who were responsible for the day-to-day program operations at each of the prisons. The skills and training required of artist-facilitators, or lead artist-teachers, would prepare them to assist community college staff and faculty. For example, artist-facilitators are responsible for coordinating arts professionals, arts organizations, and vendors, as well as recruiting, training, and evaluating artist-teachers. They also need to have general knowledge of the goals and objectives of a multidisciplinary arts program to develop a plan that meets the needs of a correctional facility.

Further, it is important that the artist-facilitator or lead artist-teacher have general knowledge of management, for example, budgets, marketing, public relations, contracts, program evaluation, planning and development, and the classroom environment. They must be knowledgeable about classroom instructional techniques and mentoring students and faculty. The ability to supervise contract artist-teachers and inmate work crews is essential as well. They must also develop and maintain cooperative relationships with institutional staff, artists, inmates, and relevant community organizations, as well as interpret and apply rules, regulations, policies, and procedures for the safety and security of the institution.

Mentoring.   Studies show that students in art programs—particularly those who are alienated from the formal education system—form positive relationships with their art instructors. Why? Perhaps their relationship is based on mutual respect as artists, rather than on authority (Dean & Field, 2003, p. 7). It is, therefore, common for artist-instructors in prison arts programs to become important mentors, offering guidance and serving as role models beyond the art room. It is reasonable to expect that this positive and motivating relationship would be extended to encouraging and assisting their students who decide to pursue a college education. This mentoring role would be particularly helpful when community college programs are offered in a distance-learning modality, such as video or online courses.

Potential for Increased Funding. A mutually supportive partnership can help to justify additional funding for the two programs. An obvious benefit for community college programs would be additional enrollments resulting from joint marketing and articulation agreements leading to college credits for approved arts courses. The reverse is true as well. Presumably, inmates will be more likely to enroll in art courses with earned college credits.

A partnership can facilitate joint lobbying efforts to persuade lawmakers, foundations, and Department of Corrections administrators to earmark additional funds in support of both programs. There is ample research evidence to suggest that the programs are natural partners in encouraging inmates to pursue higher education, and in the process, developing life-effective skills, self-confidence, discipline, and a work ethic to succeed outside prison walls. There are many Leons in prison who are eager for the opportunity to find their hidden talents and learn the pleasure and satisfaction found through completing projects.

Summing Up

There are many reasons why community colleges and prison arts organizations should explore partnerships to advance their respective missions and goals in service to the incarcerated. Compelling evidence suggests that the artistic process and arts education help motivate and prepare inmates for academic and vocational programs. Interdisciplinary research, for example, shows that training in music, poetry, creative writing, visual, or performing arts is correlated with improved interpersonal, critical thinking, and verbal skills. Prison arts education helps inmates develop a disciplined work ethic and enjoy a greater sense of self-worth, competence, and accomplishment. These life-effectiveness skills are the essential building blocks for success in academic studies, and in life after prison.

Community colleges are the backbone of higher education in the United States. They serve nearly half of all undergraduate students at reasonable cost, and offer a wide range of academic and vocational courses to a diverse student population in urban, suburban, and rural locations. Community colleges are in many important ways the perfect provider of higher education to prisoners. The open-door mission, flexible curriculum, institutional accreditation necessary to qualify for Department of Education Grants to States for Workplace and Community Training for prisoners, and broad geographical distribution make them the perfect provider of higher education in prisons, as evidenced by the growing number of community colleges offering academic and vocational programs in correctional facilities (Office of Vocational and Adult Education, 2009).

There are also increasing numbers of nonprofit organizations delivering arts education inside the walls. The ultimate, shared, goal of these academic and arts programs is to prepare inmates for reintegration back into society, thereby reducing recidivism. These programs are particularly important when we consider that inmates are less educated than the general population, and those who have earned college credits or degrees are much less likely to return to prison once released.

A dynamic collaboration between community colleges and prison arts programs will contribute to greater efficiencies and resources for both programs while encouraging better prepared inmates to pursue their education. A partnership would facilitate recruitment of inmate-artists into associate's degree programs by developing a mutually agreed upon program of study, granting college credit for art courses taught by qualified artist-instructors, and sharing staff responsibilities for recruiting and advising students, training and assisting faculty in navigating prison rules and regulations, and the myriad other tasks required of staff.

Prison arts program evaluations have found that artist-instructors often serve as important mentors, especially for the many inmates who as children and adolescents struggled in school. One reason inmate-artists form positive relationships with their art instructors is that they experience the instructor as an artist, and not so much as an authority figure. As mentors and role models, artist-instructors may play an important role in encouraging their students to advance their education in partnership with a community college.

A national trend is to look to public, private, and nonprofit partnerships as a possible solution for many of the intractable problems confronting the country today. Community colleges and prison arts organizations are one example of a partnership that can result in a more efficient and effective delivery of educational services to inmates eager to acquire life-effectiveness skills and a college education.

It is time we teach inmates how to live in the outside world, rather than simply exist on the inside. In her insightful book *The New Jim Crow*, Michelle Alexander (2010) writes that the one thing prisons do create is more inmates. She refers to a National Advisory Commission on Criminal Justice Standards and Goals report that argued, "The prison, the reformatory and the jail have achieved only a shocking record of failure. There is overwhelming evidence that these institutions create crime rather than prevent

NEW DIRECTIONS FOR COMMUNITY COLLEGES • DOI: 10.1002/cc

it." A partnership between prison arts and community college programs is one path toward self-discovery and preparation for a successful transition from prison life to life after incarceration.

References

Alexander, M. (2010). *The new Jim Crow: Mass incarceration in the age of colorblindness.* New York, NY: The New Press.

Blacker, J., Watson, A., & Beech, A. R. (2008). A combined drama-based and CBT approach to working with self-reported anger aggression. *Criminal Behavior and Mental Health, 18,* 129–137.

Brewster, L. (2012a). Arts-in-Corrections: A path of discovery and redemption. In C. Argenio, D. Owens, & J. Chin (Eds.), *Contemporary issues in criminal justice: A research-based introduction* (pp. 275–291). Flushing, NY: Looseleaf Law Publications.

Brewster, L. (2012b). *Qualitative study of the California Arts-in-Corrections program.* Retrieved from http://cac.ca.gov/arts-in-corrections/LegHearingMay2013/4-research%20a.%20brewster.pdf

Brewster, L. (2014). *California prison arts: A quantitative evaluation.* William James Association website. Retrieved from http://williamjamesassociation.org/california-prison-arts-evaluation-2014/

Clements, P. (2004). The rehabilitative role of arts education in prison: Accommodation or enlightenment? *The International Journal of Art & Design Education, 23*(2), 169–178.

Dean, C., & Field, J. (2003). *Building lives through an artistic community.* IFECSA Conference 2003, Australasian Corrections Education Association, Inc. Retrieved from http://www.acea.org.au/Content/2003%20papers/Paper%20Dean_Field.pdf

Directorate General for Education and Culture, European Commission. (2011). *Prison education and training in Europe—A review and commentary of existing literature, analysis and evaluation.* Retrieved from http://ec.europa.eu/justice/news/consulting_public/0012/Fullreport_en.pdf

Gussak, D., & Ploumis-Devick, E. (2004). Creating wellness in corrections populations through the arts: An interdisciplinary model. *Visual Arts Research, 29*(1), 35–43.

Hearing of the Joint Committee on the Arts. (2013, May 3). *Undereducate–overincarcerate: Can the arts help to turn this around?* Chaired by State Senator Curren D. Price, Jr., Chair. The Clive Davis Theater, Los Angeles, CA.

Henri, R. (2007). *The art spirit.* New York, NY: Basic Books.

Jiang, S., & Winfree, T. (2006). Social support, gender, and inmate adjustment to prison life: Insights from a national sample. *The Prison Journal, 86,* 32–55. Retrieved from http://tpj.sagepub.com/cgi/content/abstract/86/1/32

Langelid, T., Maki, M., Raundrup, K., & Svensson, S. (Eds.). (2009). *Nordic prison education: A lifelong learning perspective* (L. Schenck, Trans.). Retrieved from: http://books.google.com/books/about/Nordic_Prison_Education.html?id=gJqO_Lzj7xgC

Office of Vocational and Adult Education. (2009). *Partnerships between community colleges and prisons: Providing workforce education and training to reduce recidivism.* Washington, DC: U.S. Department of Education.

Sautter, R. C. (1994). An arts education school reform strategy. *Phi Delta Kappan, 75*(6), 432–437.

Silber, L. (2005). Bars behind bars: The impact of a women's prison choir on social harmony. *Music Education Research, 7*(2), 251–271.

Stevens, V. (2000). *The importance of creativity, emotional intelligence and the arts for education in the 21st century.* Presented at the National Academy of Recording

Arts and Sciences. Retrieved from http://drvictoriastevens.com/publications/stevens
_edu21update2000.pdf

Winner, E., & Hetland, L. (2007, September 2). Art for our sake: School arts classes matter more than ever—But not for the reasons you think. *The Boston Globe*, p. 1. Retrieved from http://www.boston.com/news/globe/ideas/articles/2007/09/02/art _for_our_sake/?page=full

Larry Brewster is a professor of public administration at the University of San Francisco, and a tireless advocate of the Arts-in-Corrections program in California state prisons.

10

In this provocative chapter, three authors engage the battle of ideas that undergird thinking about prison today, and they call for a reconceptualization of prison education in terms of a participatory model rather than thinking of it as a "service."

College Civic Engagement and Education Behind Bars: Connecting Communities, Creating Change

Mary Rachel Gould, Gillian Harkins, Kyes Stevens

Higher education, once prevalent in prisons throughout the United States, is now considered "radical" or "unnecessary" programming in the punitive model of justice that arose in the later decades of the 20th century. As the introduction to this volume suggests and as we briefly describe throughout this chapter, higher education programs in prison have been transformed by changes in federal and state policies related to higher education and incarceration, predominantly the elimination of Pell grants for incarcerated men and women.[1] In the aftermath of these changes, higher-education-in-prison programs face an uphill battle in justifying their work to a number of different audiences. They must raise funds to fill in the tuition gaps left by Pell grant removal and often to support even basic staffing and infrastructure needs. They must convince college administrators of the importance of providing higher education for students who are currently incarcerated, the Department of Corrections that higher-education-in-prison programs do not interfere with their new punitive mandate, and the broader voting and tax-paying public that higher-education-in-prison programs are not "rewarding" people who have committed crimes with "free" college. This creates a paradox for higher education programs in prison: In order to survive, they are often pressed to justify their work in ways that contradict each other or minimize the goal of higher education as a basic human right.

This chapter addresses the paradox of higher education in prison by proposing a participatory education model in which the teaching and learning practices of higher education inside prison are transformed into platforms for public education and outreach for colleges. We understand this

NEW DIRECTIONS FOR COMMUNITY COLLEGES, no. 170, Summer 2015 © 2015 Wiley Periodicals, Inc.
Published online in Wiley Online Library (wileyonlinelibrary.com) • DOI: 10.1002/cc.20148

model as part of broader multisectorial efforts to decrease reliance on incarceration to solve social problems linked to inequity, to provide high-quality public education prior to incarceration, and to interrupt what is now called the "Cradle-to-Prison" pipeline funneling many youth away from school and into juvenile and adult carceral spaces. We see colleges as key players in prison higher education because of their mission to serve diverse and often under-resourced local community members. This chapter, written through the experiences of three educators and activists working and teaching within U.S. prisons, takes up only one part of a multisectorial approach to education justice: the need to provide access to higher education for people who are currently incarcerated and to transform the justification of education to include broader human, intellectual, and social outcomes. To address this need, we propose a participatory education model that centers currently incarcerated students in the remaking of effective community and college partnerships.

The Paradox of Higher Education in Prison

It is difficult to measure the social costs of not educating the incarcerated, just as it is impossible to quantify lost dreams. In tangible terms, studies document the economic costs in terms of lack of employment and underemployment. According to the National Center for Education Statistics (NCES), the median income of persons ages 18–67 who had not completed high school was roughly $23,000 in 2008 (Rouse, 2007). By comparison, according to the NCES, in 2011, persons aged 18–67 who completed at least an associate's degree could expect to earn $37,000, and $44,900 with a bachelor's degree. Over a lifetime, this could translate into a loss of approximately $650,000 in income for a person who did not complete high school compared with someone with at least two years of college ("Income of Young Adults," n.d.).[2] Yet while the findings continue to suggest that a direct link can be established between the benefits of education in prison and success in the community, prisons in the United States more and more resemble education deserts where often the highest level of attainment a person can achieve is a GED.

In many states, even vocational training and GED programs are treated as luxuries that the incarcerated do not deserve. State governments and, more likely, Departments of Corrections (DOCs) that allow prison education programs in their facilities most often partner with local universities and colleges, in many cases community colleges, to offer for-credit and not-for-credit courses and programs and are funded by the academic institution. We stress the need to engage community colleges because, as institutions, they are already working with nontraditional student populations, including distance learning, first-generation students, and students needing college preparation courses. In addition, the cost and in some cases locations of these colleges are less prohibitive to currently incarcerated students. In the current climate of retribution and not rehabilitation, few men and women are given the opportunity to leave the prison system with the educational or life-skill resources necessary to integrate back into the community.

At the same time, those education programs in prison that are at least attempting to provide basic requirements for students are put in the position of working with a population that often enters the system with severely lower educational attainment and academic readiness than the general population. According to one study, an estimated "40% of State prison inmates, 27% of Federal inmates, 47% of inmates in local jails, and 31% of those serving probation sentences had not completed high school or its equivalent" (Harlow, 2003, p. 2). According to Harlow (2003), these findings are in stark contrast to the general population where approximately 18% have failed to attain high school graduation. Over the past 30 years, rates of incarceration in the United States have grown significantly for men and women without a high school diploma or equivalent, as the average state inmate has a 10th-grade education (Western, 2006; Western & Pettit, 2010). Because it is estimated that 95% of the more than 2 million men and women currently held in U.S. prisons and jails will be released, opportunities for higher education are critical, and it is the explicit argument of this chapter that education, and particularly a model of participatory education, is vital to the success of the currently and formerly incarcerated. While a multisectorial approach is needed to provide greater access to education, skills, and jobs prior to entry into the carceral system, higher education programs inside prisons can help decrease reliance on incarceration for problems linked to educational equity and improve life chances for those who have already ended up in the system.

Yet DOC funding for education programming inside prisons remains scarce, and many programs rely upon the labor (paid or volunteer) of educators from local colleges and universities. In particular, community colleges have played a key role in filling the gaps left by this systemic shift in relations between access to higher education and routing through carceral institutions. Because many of these colleges, as part of public school districts, are eligible for CTE credits, they are often better poised to assume the financial impact of creating and sustaining a prison higher education program.[3] Some colleges formally contract with correctional institutions to provide specific educational programming. In Washington State, for example, colleges hold exclusive contracts with the DOC to provide mandatory GED coursework and some vocational classes (state law prohibits using public money to provide a broader range of higher education opportunities for incarcerated students). The administration of such programs operates through DOC in conjunction with the college administration. The DOC provides access to prisons, volunteer training, facilities, and staff time to support educational programs. College personnel provide facilitation of coursework, student assessment, recordkeeping, and academic/degree accreditation and credentials. In addition to the labor involved on the part of these two institutions, volunteer or nonprofit staff may provide intermediary labor and assistance in creating and maintaining these institutional partnerships.

One key problem that emerges for higher education programs in prison run by private or state colleges and universities is how to build relationships among institutions when each has a very different mission and rationale for its practices. Community colleges, because of their mission to educate the most underresourced members of a community, can be a corrective to these obstacles. Yet, even while colleges tend to focus on the fundamental good of higher education and the institutions' stated mission to increase educational access for all students, the DOCs tend to focus on the link between access to higher education inside prisons and their stated mission to increase public safety and decrease recidivism (rates of return) upon release from prison. A paradox still remains that may make it difficult for higher education programs in prison to create messages that honor their own mission and aims while also garnering support from institutions with divergent missions and aims. To resolve this paradox, programs often rely on a "service" model of higher education in prison to address to both college and prison audiences. This rationale suggests that higher education programs in prison deliver a "service" that enhances the college's mission to provide education to historically excluded or underserved communities and the DOC's mission to provide rehabilitative programs to those they imprison.

Building Effective Partnerships

Instead of the current service-oriented model, prison higher education might be better presented as a collaborative or what we consider a *participatory model*—with educators across the university, including undergraduates, staff, and faculty, working with educators behind bars, including incarcerated students and nonprofit staff, to facilitate this effort. Foremost in this conversation, we believe it is critical for colleges to view higher education programs in prison as a key part of their overall education and community engagement strategy and as an opportunity to adapt enrollment strategies targeting nontraditional (off-campus) students, instead of a small service opportunity for a few instructors. A participatory model of education shifts familiar ways of identifying and differentiating teaching and service and helps reconsider how colleges understand their relationship to community publics.

To begin to build the infrastructure to facilitate participatory models, it is necessary to bring together two relatively unfamiliar entities—the college and the DOC. Building a prison higher education program requires great determination because of the societal and institutional stigma projected onto people in prisons. If you choose to do this work, you must cast a wide net and build diverse partnerships so that all the relevant institutions and communities see value and contribute to the outreach and engagement initiatives of the program. For anyone considering developing such programming, your partnerships within your college and with the DOC are crucial in determining the success of your program. For many prison higher education programs, it takes years of work to create a secure foundation. One approach that cannot be underestimated is the extraordinary value of face time with individuals. While it might save time and money to e-mail or make a phone call, to build lasting relationships with any community, and especially a community vastly different from your own, you must venture forth and learn about the people and the dynamics that influence them. To be equal partners and investors in higher-education-in-prison programs, avenues of dialogue must be open and frank. Do not walk in and pronounce that you and your program hold the magic key for fixing any "problem," especially a crisis as great as the education void in the prison system. Do not assume that you have support from either your college/university or the DOC; spend equal time building a strong relationship with the administration and faculty on campus as well as the DOC and local prison administration.

Developing strong relationships with the communities served by the sponsoring college is also key to achieving participatory goals. Your local college administration may question your focus, intentions, and vision in creating a prison higher education program, especially in an era of dwindling budgets and positioning for scarce resources. Even at colleges where there is overwhelming institutional support for a higher education program in prison, there are still significant questions about where the work of facilitating such a program fits into the community-focused college model. Part of the work of everyone involved in a higher education program in prison is ensuring that conversations exist that address how the college defines and meets the needs of its communities. This can be achieved by building solid partnerships with community leaders and community-based groups working for education justice in your region and supporting community leadership among those who are currently incarcerated and those seeking educational opportunities after release. The success of a program can only come as a result of the unwavering cooperation between community partners, college administrators, and faculty and staff who support programs financially, politically, and through acts of goodwill.

In an effort to begin thinking about the most effective ways to create participatory models for higher education programs in prison, we offer some advice based upon our experiences working and teaching within U.S. prisons. As such, we advocate for an approach to prison higher education based upon collaboration, communication, determination, and compassion.

Collaborate with people inside and outside the prison system about how to set realistic, achievable goals and continue to partner to determine what a higher education program inside prison is designed to achieve, who should be involved in its design, and how and why it should be sustained.

Seek out and listen to people who have been or are currently incarcerated about their experience with and expectations for higher education, people who have been working within the prison system to create and sustain similar programs, and people who have been working within the university/college system to create programs reaching traditionally underserved students. Collaboration will also help you avoid the most dangerous mistake that can be made in well-intentioned efforts to increase incarcerated access to higher education: setting goals based on low expectations. When you work in isolation, it is easy to believe that something is better than nothing or that anything you do is intrinsically beneficial. When you collaborate, you are held accountable to the best practices already in existence and can ask for support to create a program that meets or exceeds the highest standards.

Communicate with constituents at your college and the DOC and facilitate opportunities for dialogue between both groups. It is likely that on the surface, the mission of your education program will not be in line with that of your state DOC or the specific facility in which you are working. It may also not be in line with the interpretation and application of the mission of your local college/university partner. Listening to each constituent is vital to the survival of your program, because it is the way you will be able to learn how to match the mission of your education program with that of your partner organizations. Asking questions and employing empathic listening—listening to improve mutual understanding—will ensure that you are working together and not against each other. It is important to keep in mind that regardless of the value of our work, we are in the facility only as long as the DOC administration allows it. In part, the success of your program will depend upon how the administration at the facility and the state DOC understand your program's relationship to their work and mission. The same can be said of the local college partner and of the community members whose lives are most entwined with and impacted by the prison system.

Be determined, have compassion, and if you are powerfully drawn to doing this work, aim steadfastly toward your goals, even if you do not have complete support from partner institutions. Start small. Be reasonable with your expectations and work toward building the solid foundation a program needs to be sustainable. The work can be slow, and you will be faced with difficult decisions that need to be assessed one step at a time. This requires you to have compassion for others as well as for yourself. As one of the authors advises, "if your heart is directing you to the work, then do it. If your heart is not 100% behind working with prisoners, then don't do it." You will also need to broaden your scope of compassion. Many people who choose to work in higher-education-in-prison programs are strongly opposed to the existing criminal justice system, but working for education inside prisons means you will encounter people working for pay inside prisons, many of whom need a job and are not in charge of the system in which they work.

The DOC and its employees will determine the success of any educational program behind bars; finding compassion for the full range of people you work with does not have to be an obstacle to having determination to accomplish the goals of participatory education.

Conclusion: Turning the Corner on Prison Higher Education

We believe the tide is turning toward greater public support for prison higher education programs. The foundation for this belief rests on the fact that some of the most conservative states in the nation, such as Texas, South Carolina, and Georgia, have recently passed prison reform bills that focus on alternatives to prisons for nonviolent offenders, as well as on the Department of Justice's recent challenge to sentencing guidelines related to nonviolent drug-related offenses. This indicates a shift away from punitive justifications for mass incarceration. For example, in 2010, South Carolina Governor Mark Sanford signed legislation enacting an overhaul of state sentencing guidelines in an effort to reduce costs and address a tripling of the South Carolina correctional population between 1985 and 2010 ("South Carolina's Public Safety Reform," 2010).[4] In recent years, Texas has also created alternatives to incarceration and is achieving significant reductions in crime while saving an estimated $2 billion in taxpayer costs that would have been spent "had Texas simply constructed more than 17,000 prison beds that a 2007 projection indicated would be needed," if they did not enact measures to reduce incarceration rates (Laudano, 2010, p. 1). The actions taken by South Carolina and Texas are representative of the ways in which states are starting to recognize and take action against the rising costs of incarceration.

Despite the growing support for programs that offer alternatives to incarceration, colleges continue to scrutinize the financial liabilities of new programming. It is important to understand how to have conversations with college administrators, DOC representatives, and the public about the financial effectiveness of prison higher education programs. The logic of punishment is ceding to or at least being modified by a logic of fiscal effectiveness. Based on the research findings outlined in the first part of this chapter, higher education in prison seems to fit well with more financially motivated rationales. Higher education programs in prison lead to better job prospects after prison and, of course, to what is most important to those passing these reform bills—turning former prisoners into taxpayers and not statistics on recidivism. But it is important not to justify claims for education solely as a preventative to recidivism and, as a result, cost reduction. As practitioners, it is vital for us to understand the full range of rationales that justify our programming. It is certain that you will often be put in the position of "defending" your program. At the same time that we recognize the value of education as a precursor to employment, prison educators must also make an argument for the value of education in its own right. Higher education in

NEW DIRECTIONS FOR COMMUNITY COLLEGES • DOI: 10.1002/cc

prison is a second chance at educational opportunities that were most likely not available prior to incarceration. Higher education in prison provides the opportunity to engage in self-discovery, the development of critical thinking skills, and the acquisition of the social and intellectual skills needed to navigate the world beyond the prison and the classroom. This type of education should be afforded to all individuals. As educators, in prison and on college campuses, we must argue that higher education is a basic human right. Participatory models, routed through higher education programs in prison, provide a key platform to make this argument.

The success and sustainability of higher education and decarceration depend upon a broader mission of public education, a conversation that can be facilitated by educators. More people need to understand the connection between our society's increasing reliance on mass incarceration and its dwindling commitment to public education. The disappearing public sphere needs to be revitalized by debates about the connections between education and incarceration—how the lack of educational resources can lead to incarceration, how a second chance at education can be achieved in prison, and how education can reduce the likelihood of reincarceration. Starting a higher-education-in-prison program puts educators at the forefront of the debate over education justice, and it is incumbent upon us as educators to willingly and effectively participate in this conversation.

This chapter is one effort to add to a much-needed dialogue on education and incarceration. Rather than warehousing humans, we need to increase our capacity to educate as a public good, as part of a shared ambition to live in a more just and equitable world, and as a way of living up to the ideal of higher education. This approach demands public scholarship, and, we argue, more participatory models of teaching and learning. Further, we encourage anyone with an interest in education justice to explore opportunities to teach in a local jail or prison. Often a program grows out of the efforts of one person. A participatory model of public scholarship brings together the intellectual contributions of those who are currently incarcerated and those on the outside who have the ability to tap into institutional resources to offer one class or a degree-granting program. Participatory education and public scholarship can effectively work to (re)educate both groups toward achieving the shared goal of creating a culture that successfully provides excellent educational opportunities for all.

Notes

1. For more on the passing and subsequent effects of the 1994 Omnibus Crime Bill, see Spearlt & Gould (2013).
2. For more on the financial repercussions of incarceration, see Rouse's (2007) work for National Center for Education Statistics (NCES).
3. See volume introduction for more on community college funding structures.
4. The plan diverts some low-risk, nonviolent offenders from prison to community-based programs. The initiative is estimated to save South Carolina $350 million. For more on the changes in South Carolina, see Wenger (2010).

References

Harlow, C. W. (2003). *Education and correctional populations*. Bureau of Justice statistics: Special Report NCJ 195670. Retrieved from http://www.bjs.gov/index.cfm?ty =pbdetail&iid=814

Income of young adults. (n.d.). *Fast facts*. Washington, DC: National Center for Education Statistics. Retrieved from http://nces.ed.gov/fastfacts/display.asp?id=77

Laudano, J. (2010). Bending the curve: Juvenile corrections reform in Texas. *Pew Center on the States Public Safety Performance Project*. Retrieved from http://www .pewstates.org/research/reports/bending-the-curve-juvenile-corrections-reform-in -texas-85899480847?p=1

Rouse, C. E. (2007). Quantifying the costs of inadequate education: Consequences of the labor market. In C. R. Belfield & H. M. Levin (Eds.), *The price we pay: Economic and social consequences of inadequate education* (pp. 99–124). Washington, DC: Brookings Institution Press.

South Carolina's public safety reform: Legislation enacts research-based strategies to cut prison growth and costs. (2010). Washington, DC: Pew Center on the States Public Safety Performance Project. Retrieved from http://www.pewtrusts.org/~/media/ Assets/2010/06/10/PSPP_South_Carolina_brief.pdf

Spearlt & Gould, M. R. (2013). 20 years after the education apocalypse: The ongoing fallout from the 1994 Omnibus Crime Bill. *Saint Louis University Public Law Review, 33*, 283–300.

Wenger, Y. (2010, June 3). New law changes criminal sentencing. *The Post and Courier*. Retrieved from http://www.postandcourier.com/article/20100603/PC1602/ 306039980

Western, B. (2006). *Punishment and inequality in America*. New York, NY: Russell Sage.

Western, B., & Pettit, B. (2010). Incarceration and social inequality. *Daealus, 139*, 8–19.

Mary Rachel Gould is an assistant professor of communication at Saint Louis University and is co-director of the Saint Louis University Prison Arts and Education Program.

Gillian Harkins is an associate professor of English at University of Washington, Seattle, and a volunteer with the University Beyond Bars, the Freedom Education Project Puget Sound, and the Black Prisoners' Caucus TEACH program.

Kyes Stevens is the founder and director of the Alabama Prison Arts and Education Project.

New Directions for Community Colleges • DOI: 10.1002/cc

INDEX

Achebe, C., 59
AGTP. *See* Attica-Genesee Teaching Project (AGTP)
Alexander, M., 2, 14, 71, 97, 98
Allen, R. L., 69, 70
Amandla!, 59, 61
Anderson, E., 73
Arts-in-Corrections, 92–93
Asante, M., 70, 73
Ashley, N., 9
Attica-Genesee Teaching Project (AGTP), 11–13

Ba, M., 59
Baca, J. S., 83
Bakeman, J., 10
Ballman, T. L., 42
Beals, M. P., 84
Beech, A. R., 91
Bell, D., 69
Bennett, L., 73
Black Boy, 83
Blacker, J., 91
Bonilla-Silva, E., 69
Bozick, R., 9, 67
Brewster, L., 6, 89–92, 99
Brookfield, S. D., 38
Bryant, A., 73
Burke, P. J., 36

Carson, E. A., 2
Chang, C., 11
Cheating/plagiarism, in prison, 51–54; violation of code, 51–53
Chemeketa Community College, 19–20
Christian, S., 9
Clarke, J. H., 72, 73
Clarke-Stewart, K. A., 9
Clements, P., 94
College Inside program. *See* Prison college program
Color of Water, The, 83
Cooper, A. D., 9
Cultural democracy, 51–54
Cureton, S., 74
Cyr, J. R., 5, 31, 40

Darder, A., 54
Davis, L. M., 9, 67
Dean, C., 96
Delaney, R., 13
Delgado, R., 69
Delpit, L., 82
DOC. *See* Oregon Department of Corrections (DOC)
Drew, J. D., 5, 31, 40
Du Bois, W. E. B., 72, 73
Durose, M. R., 9
Duval, J., 5, 31, 40
Dyson, M., 73

Ehrenreich, B., 84
Elizabeth and Hazel: Two Women of Little Rock, 84
Enrique's Journey, 83
Espenshade, T. J., 15
Ethnic studies, in prison: African history course, 58–63; commitment and creativity in, 64; community building in, 62–63; identity development in, 60–61; overview, 57–58; sustainability of, 64; use of liberation pedagogy in, 63–64

Farley, A., 42
Field, J., 96
Fine arts programs, in prison: community college and, 94–96; description of, 91–94; intersection with academic programs, 90–91; mentoring in, 95–96; outcomes of, 91; overview, 89–90; proposed program of study, 94–95; recruitment of students for, 94; shared administrative responsibilities in, 95
Forbes, C., 69
Foster, M., 69, 70
Frazier, F. E., 72, 74
Freire, P., 38, 63

Garvey, A. J., 74
Garvey, M., 72
Gaskew, T., 6, 67, 72, 73, 78
GCC. *See* Genesee Community College (GCC)

111

CC169 Dual Enrollment Policies, Pathways, and Perspectives
Jason L. Taylor, Joshua Pretlow
Dual enrollment is an expanding program that allows high school students to
accrue college credits prior to high school graduation. Advocates of dual
enrollment point to the financial and academic benefits of dual enrollment,
and accumulating research suggests dual enrollment has a positive impact on
students' access to and success in college. In this volume of *New Directions
for Community Colleges*, aspects of dual enrollment practices and policies will
be explained, including:

• state policies that regulate dual enrollment practice and the influence of
  state policy on local practice,
• the usage of dual enrollment programs as a pathway for different
  populations of students such as career and technical education students
  and students historically underrepresented in higher education, and
• chapters that surface student, faculty, and high school stakeholder
  perspectives and that examine institutional and partnership performance
  and quality.

This volume addresses issues and topics critical for community college
leaders, administrators, and policymakers to engage in and understand as
they develop new dual enrollment programs or adapt and revamp existing
dual enrollment programs.
ISBN: 978-11190-54184

CC168 Budget and Finance in the American Community College
Trudy H. Bers, Ronald B. Head, James C. Palmer
The literature about budgets and finance in community colleges is
surprisingly sparse and most is dated. In this volume of *New Directions for
Community Colleges*, key issues and practices will be addressed on the
following topics:

• the contemporary challenge of meeting growing demands for increased
  student persistence and success,
• diminishing state support for higher education,
• new calls for accountability and ways to measure institutional effectiveness,
• the increasing reliance of many community colleges on grants and other
  sources of revenue, and
• college policies that have significant financial ramifications.

The intended audience for this volume includes community college
leaders, new administrators, board members, budget and finance staff, and
faculty and students in higher education and community college graduate
programs. The volume may also be a useful overview for budget and finance
leaders such as chief financial officers.
ISBN: 978-11190-41566

NEW DIRECTIONS FOR COMMUNITY COLLEGE
ORDER FORM SUBSCRIPTION AND SINGLE ISSUES

DISCOUNTED BACK ISSUES:

Use this form to receive 20% off all back issues of *New Directions for Community College*.
All single issues priced at **$23.20** (normally $29.00)

TITLE	ISSUE NO.	ISBN

Call 1-800-835-6770 or see mailing instructions below. When calling, mention the promotional code JBNND to receive your discount. For a complete list of issues, please visit www.josseybass.com/go/ndcc

SUBSCRIPTIONS: (1 YEAR, 4 ISSUES)

☐ New Order   ☐ Renewal

U.S.	☐ Individual: $89	☐ Institutional: $335
CANADA/MEXICO	☐ Individual: $89	☐ Institutional: $375
ALL OTHERS	☐ Individual: $113	☐ Institutional: $409

Call 1-800-835-6770 or see mailing and pricing instructions below.
Online subscriptions are available at www.onlinelibrary.wiley.com

ORDER TOTALS:

Issue / Subscription Amount: $ _____

Shipping Amount: $ _____
(for single issues only – subscription prices include shipping)

Total Amount: $ _____

SHIPPING CHARGES:

First Item	$6.00
Each Add'l Item	$2.00

(No sales tax for U.S. subscriptions. Canadian residents, add GST for subscription orders. Individual rate subscriptions must be paid by personal check or credit card. Individual rate subscriptions may not be resold as library copies.)

BILLING & SHIPPING INFORMATION:

☐ **PAYMENT ENCLOSED:** *(U.S. check or money order only. All payments must be in U.S. dollars.)*

☐ **CREDIT CARD:** ☐ VISA ☐ MC ☐ AMEX

Card number _____ Exp. Date _____

Card Holder Name _____ Card Issue # _____

Signature _____ Day Phone _____

☐ **BILL ME:** *(U.S. institutional orders only. Purchase order required.)*

Purchase order # _____
Federal Tax ID 13559302 • GST 89102-8052

Name _____

Address _____

Phone _____ E-mail _____

Copy or detach page and send to: **John Wiley & Sons, One Montgomery Street, Suite 1000, San Francisco, CA 94104-4594**

Order Form can also be faxed to: **888-481-2665**

PROMO JBNND